CLARK
2003

D0130753

Rethinking the Great Depression

RETHINKING THE GREAT DEPRESSION

Gene Smiley

The American Ways Series

IVAN R. DEE   *Chicago*

Library of Congress Cataloging-in-Publication Data:
Smiley, Gene, 1940–
    Rethinking the Great Depression / Gene Smiley.
        p. cm. — (American ways series)
    Includes bibliographical references and index.
        ISBN 1-56663-472-5 (cloth : alk. paper) — ISBN 1-56663-471-7
(paper : alk. paper)
        1. Depressions—1929. 2. Economic history—1918–1945. 3.
Business cycles—History—20th century. 4. Depressions—1929—
United States. 5. United States—Economic policy—1933–1945. 6.
New Deal, 1933–1939. I. Title. II. Series.

HB3717 1929 .S55 2002
330.973'0917—dc21   2002023761

To Sam Williamson and Joe Swanson
who led me into economic history

Contents

Preface

THE GREAT DEPRESSION was the single most important economic event in the twentieth century. No depression before or since has been so severe and so long. The recovery from it was extraordinarily slow and painful. It ushered in changes in the role of the federal government that continue to this day, and it shook the faith of many people in market economies, and, in many ways, created conditions that led to World War II.

In the years since the 1930s we have come to know much more about the nature of the economic contraction, the reasons why it occurred, and why the recovery was so delayed. But much of this recent scholarship on the 1930s has not made its way into formats more accessible to the nonspecialist. In this brief work I intend to survey the 1930s so that readers without training in economics have a better understanding of the forces at work in the period between the two world wars.

I use the economist's identification of the Great Depression: it was the contraction phase that ran from the early summer of 1929 to the end of the first quarter of 1933. The economy slowly and haltingly recovered between March 1933 and May 1937 when, even though full employment had not been restored, another depression occurred. The recovery from this depression lasted from May 1938 until at least the entry of the United States into World War II. The first chapter describes the prosperous twenties and contrasts that to the depression of the early thirties. The second chapter explains why the Great Depression occurred and why it was so long and so severe. The necessary economic tools for this analysis are presented in the first part of this chapter. The next two chapters examine the different segments of the recovery from the Great Depression and look at the reasons for the slowness of the recovery. The final chapter examines World War II and the legacy of the Great Depression.

Those readers who have not been introduced to recent scholarship on the subject may find some surprising conclusions. The Great Depression is often said to demonstrate the instability of market economies and the need for government oversight and direction. The evidence can no longer support such assumptions. Government efforts to control and direct the gold standard for national purposes brought on the depression. Once it began, government actions, particularly in the United States, caused it to be much longer and much more severe. When the contraction finally ended, government interference in U.S. markets made the recovery unbearably slow and in 1937–1938 brought on a "depression within a depression." The 1930s economic crisis is tragic testimony to government interference in market economies.

This book draws upon the research of economists and economic historians who are too numerous to mention. There are, however, specific debts that I must acknowledge. Richard H. Keehn of the University of Wisconsin-Parkside read all of the chapter drafts of this book and offered extensive and constructive, but encouraging, criticisms. Lawrence Malone of Hartwick College also commented on most of the chapters. Michael Upton, Toby Bates, Brian Craig Miller, and Michael V. Namorato of the University of Mississippi offered valuable comments on the first three draft chapters. Mark Skousen, president of the Foundation for Economic Education, also provided important suggestions. Robert Higgs of the Independent Institute, on whose work I have drawn extensively, encouraged me to pursue this project, though he did not read draft chapters and bears no responsibility for their content.

The timely completion of the book would not have been possible without the generous support of the Social Philosophy and Policy Center at Bowling Green State University in Bowling Green, Ohio. An appointment as a visiting research scholar for the two months of June and July 2001 allowed me to devote all my time to completing the research and writing of this book. The center graciously provided me with an office and computer and obtained any materials I needed while working on the book. Discussions with Jeff Paul, Travis Cook, and Fred Miller of the Social Philosophy and Policy Center helped clarify ideas and pointed me in the direction of additional materials.

My development of this book was also aided by two Liberty Fund weekend conferences on the Great Depression. The first, in June 2001 at Milwaukee, Wisconsin, undertook a re-examination of Murray Rothbard's, *America's Great Depression*. The second, in October 2001 at San Jose, California, examined liberty and the Great Depression and helped me come to grips with several ideas I was considering. The roundtable discussions over Friday and Saturday at both conferences helped clarify many points. I owe a considerable debt to the participants of those two seminars.

The largest debt is owed to John Braeman of the University of Nebraska, the editor of this series, who painstakingly read every draft, corrected my notoriously poor writing, noted factual inaccuracies, and pointed out reorganizations of the book to better develop and present my ideas.

If I have not always followed the suggestions of the readers listed above, that is certainly no fault of theirs. They cannot be held responsible for the remaining errors, but the book is immeasurably better because of their suggestions.

Finally I must acknowledge my wife, Carol Smiley. She has done more of the chores around our home than she should have because I protested that I was too busy working on the book. She remained in Milwaukee for June and July 2001 while I spent all my time at the Social Philosophy and Policy Center writing and reading. Some debts can never be repaid.

G. S.

Waukesha, Wisconsin
April 2002

Rethinking the Great Depression

1

Prosperity Gives Way to the Great Depression

ON MONDAY, March 4, 1929, in the midst of a drizzling rain, Herbert Clark Hoover took the oath of office as president of the United States. In his inaugural address he waxed enthusiastic about the nation under the Republican administrations of the 1920s. The United States had achieved a higher degree of comfort than had ever existed anywhere on earth. In fact, according to Hoover, it had been liberated from widespread poverty. During the 1928 presidential campaign a Republican brochure promised a chicken in every pot and a car in every garage. Such glowing promises of what the public could expect under a Hoover administration were not considered at all outlandish.

By the early summer of 1929, however, economic activity in the United States was noticeably slowing. The economic contraction continued to spread through the rest of the summer and into the fall of 1929. In the last week of October the stock market "crashed" and economic activity declined more rapidly. The depression that had begun in the early summer of 1929 dragged on for four years, and it became clear that rather than a "liberation from widespread poverty," the condition had spread further into American society. Recovery from the

Great Depression was so slow that the entire decade of the 1930s is often referred to as the Great Depression. It is the only decade in the history of the United States in which there was no economic growth. Income per person in 1939—adjusted for changes in the general level of prices, or *real* income per person—was less than in 1929.

Economic Growth in the Twenties

Hoover's characterization of the United States economy in early 1929 and his promises of what were to come were not unrealistic. The country had made substantial real economic gains during the 1920s. Where automobile companies had produced 1,658,000 cars in 1919, production had nearly tripled to 4,587,000 cars by 1929. In 1919 there were 1.12 cars registered for every four households in the United States; ten years later there were 3.15 cars registered for every four households. With this rise in car ownership and a growing number of used cars, there was every reason to think that within a reasonably short time most families could own an automobile. And Hoover's "chicken in every pot" promise accurately reflected the growth of incomes during the previous decade. Between 1923 and 1929 real income per person (measured as Gross National Product per capita in 1929 dollars) increased 12.6 percent, from $763 to $859—or, if calculated on an annual basis, by 2.1 percent per year. The population of the country increased from 111.9 million to 121.8 million during those same years. Other measures also point to strong real economic growth during the 1920s. Between 1923 and 1929, the real average annual earnings of employees increased 15.7 percent as real wage rates rose. Manufacturing production increased 23.5 percent between 1923 and 1929 while productivity (output per man-hour) rose nearly 14 percent over the same period.

The American economy did not simply produce more of the same things—it produced many new products and services. A key to much of this growth was the spreading use of commercially generated electricity. Electricity was the basis for a great many other new consumer products such as refrigerators, phonographs, electric irons, electric fans, electric lighting, toasters, vacuum cleaners, and other household appliances. To deliver electricity to homes, electric utility companies were created for the generation and transmission of electric power. Radios and radio stations first appeared in the early twenties and quickly became an important source of news and entertainment as they began to break the isolation of rural life. By the mid-twenties the first national radio networks appeared, and by the end of the decade there were three of them. The new RCA (Radio Corporation of America) was one of the highest-flying stocks in the stock market boom of the late twenties.

Rising incomes and slowly declining workweeks, along with the convenience of the automobile, led to a revolution in leisure activities. The explosion of movie theaters and the development of Hollywood can also be attributed to the expanded use of electricity. Professional sports became a big business, drawing large crowds. More people began to travel regularly, and motor hotels (or motels) and roadside diners that catered to the motoring crowd became common. Greater automobile use led to an expanded program of paved road construction to accommodate increasing numbers of motorists. Cities had to post policemen to direct traffic at intersections and finally began to install electric traffic signals to regulate the crush of city traffic. Suburbs sprang up around cities as the automobile allowed greater ease and flexibility in getting to work. Jitneys (unlicensed taxis) and then taxis competed with the fixed-rail mass transit systems that larger cities had created. Sears, Roebuck and Montgomery Ward, the two largest mail order (or catalog) firms, opened retail stores on major streets leading to the downtown areas of cities in order to take advantage of growing automobile traffic and the movement of population away from city centers.

Rising incomes and production were brought about by sustained gains in productivity in agriculture and manufacturing. The development of the gasoline-powered tractor paralleled the development of the car and the truck. Mechanization on the farm increased when the versatile row-crop tractor appeared in the mid-twenties and the average size of family farms began growing. In manufacturing, increases in productivity reduced the unit costs of products. Henry Ford had pioneered the development of the moving assembly line in 1913, which changed the nature of manufacturing. Production of Model T Fords at the Highland Park, Michigan, factory rose from 78,000 to 248,000 annually with the full introduction of moving assembly lines in Ford's plant. These gains in productivity were dramatic, and Ford's profits increased sharply. But work on the assembly lines was hard, and labor turnover was high. When Ford used his additional profits to offer profit-sharing for eligible employees, effectively doubling the wage rate to five dollars per day, his problem of high labor turnover disappeared.

During the 1920s moving assembly-line technology spread to other automobile producers and into the production of many other types of products. By the mid-twenties Ford's new River Rouge plant was producing nearly 1.8 million Model T Fords each year, and the price of the Model T—$600 in 1912—had fallen to $240. In 1929 Ford and Chevrolet alone produced almost 2.5 million cars. A crucial factor in this productivity growth was the increasing use of electricity in manufacturing. Machinery could be powered by smaller independent electric motors, allowing production to be rearranged in a more rational manner as manufacturing was freed from the constraints imposed by steam or waterpower. Time and motion studies pioneered by Frederick Taylor and others (including Ford) helped increase worker productivity. Thousands of other continuing improvements led to ongoing increases in productivity and rising incomes for most of the population.

PROBLEM AREAS IN THE TWENTIES

Some areas of the economy were having more difficult times during the general expansion of the 1920s. Grain farmers faced uncertain markets. During and immediately after World War I, farming—primarily grain farming—had expanded as increases in overseas demand led to rapidly rising prices. Farm prospects appeared excellent in the heady days from 1917 into 1919, so farmers borrowed to purchase additional land and machinery, and lenders were generally happy to lend them what they asked for because the security for the loans, the value of the farmland, was rising rapidly. Cash-strapped farmers frequently took out second mortgages to obtain the bulk of their down payment. But the good times did not last. European agricultural production recovered quickly after the war, and by early 1920 agricultural prices—especially grain prices—were being driven downward by huge declines in overseas demand for American foodstuffs. The United States endured a sharp but mercifully short depression between mid-1920 and mid-1921. Where wholesale and consumer prices had risen between 1919 and 1920, consumer prices fell 11.3 percent between 1920 and 1921 while wholesale prices fell nearly 46 percent. Agricultural prices as a whole declined slightly between 1919 and 1920 and then, led by grain prices, plummeted 53.3 percent between 1920 and 1921. Although grain prices recovered somewhat by the mid-twenties, they never approached the levels of 1917–1919. Farmers' real debt burdens increased dramatically as farm prices and income fell but debt remained fixed. The 1920s witnessed a continuing series of farm foreclosures while prices for farmland, the supposedly safe security, continued to decline.

The coal industry also failed to share in the general prosperity. Too much productive capacity and declining demand plagued the industry. Low prices meant low incomes and uncertain employment for miners. Technological improvements allowed coal users, such as electric utilities, manufacturing, home heating, and steam engines, to use less coal while obtaining as much or more energy. Competition increased from electricity, oil, and gasoline and contributed to reductions in the price of coal. The old-line textile and shoe industries also suffered from slow growth and declining profits. For workers in those industries, adjustment and relocation were often slow and painful. Still, these problem areas did not detract from the overall prosperity of the 1920s, a period of rapid technological change and the appearance of new products and new processes. In such dynamic periods some industries grow while others decline and these industries simply happened to be some of those that naturally declined in the 1920s.

Taxes, Income Distribution, and the Stock Market Boom

In 1913 the federal government imposed a modest but slightly progressive personal income tax. With this revenue structure in place, Washington used the income tax as a major source of additional taxes to finance its role in World War I. In 1914 the lowest rate was 1 percent on net incomes of $4,000 to $6,000. By 1918 the lowest rate had risen to 6 percent on net incomes from $2,000 to $4,000. The highest rate in 1914 was 7 percent on all income in excess of $750,000. By 1918 individuals with net incomes in excess of $750,000 paid 76 percent of their income above $750,000 to the government. Income tax rates were reduced somewhat at the end of the war and, though there was general agreement that rates should be further reduced, the size and nature of the reductions was in dispute. Democrats and progressive Republicans argued for smaller reductions concentrated in lower-income taxpayers. Secretary of the Treasury Andrew Mellon and other Republicans argued that there was widespread legal tax avoidance by higher-income taxpayers and that only a general rate reduction, particularly for high-income taxpayers who faced high marginal tax rates, would alleviate the problem.

Unable to find effective ways to plug tax loopholes, Congress finally reduced the highest rate to 25 percent on net incomes over $100,000. The lowest rate was reduced to 2 percent on net incomes between $2,000 and $6,000, but increased personal exemptions sharply reduced the number of taxpayers in the $2,000 to $6,000 net income class. The federal government enjoyed budget surpluses throughout the 1920s, and these surpluses remained even when tax rates were cut. The share of the total federal income tax burden borne by the highest taxpayers rose throughout the decade despite the fact that they enjoyed the largest absolute tax rate cuts.

In 1924 common stock prices began rising, and in 1925 the Standard and Poor's common stock index surpassed its 1916 peak. Stock prices continued to rise in the late twenties as one of the great speculative stock market booms in history unfolded. In some ways the stock market mirrored the rise of skyscrapers, such as Minneapolis's Foshay Tower, Chicago's Wrigley Building and Tribune Tower, and New York City's Chrysler Building and Empire State Building. Just as the depression ended skyscraper construction until the 1950s, so did the stock market cash in October 1929 signal the end of the speculative booms of the 1920s. The first surge in farmland prices at the end of World War I was followed in the mid-

1920s by a spectacular boom in Florida real estate centered in
the Miami area. This bubble burst with the 1926 hurricane
and supply bottlenecks that choked the railroads and ships
bringing supplies to Miami. But the stock market boom more
than made up for the Florida collapse as stock prices soared in
1928 and 1929 before they crashed in the fall of 1929.

Until the collapse, the stock market took Americans on a
dizzying ride. Stock prices and the daily volume of shares
traded continued to set records in the late twenties. The rise
was interrupted several times by price breaks and dire predic-
tions of the end of the bull market, but each time the market
recovered. New securities were issued as merger activity accelerated and holding companies were formed to take advantage of rising stock prices. Large American corporations
began lending money to Wall Street brokers to enable them to
make margin loans—where buyers of securities put up 20 or
30 percent of the purchase price of the security and borrowed
the rest from the broker—as interest rates on margin loans
rose. In some cases the interest on margin loans exceeded the
corporation's expected returns on new investment projects.

There are no definitive answers to why the boom started or
why it gathered such strength at the end of the decade. In the
first half of the 1920s common stocks appear to have been un-
derpriced. As firms adopted policies that paid stockholders
stable dividends, and as corporate profits rose, common stock
prices were bid up. In 1924 and 1927 the nation's central bank,
the Federal Reserve System, engineered temporarily lower interest rates which helped to boost stock prices. Anticipated
corporate profits grew, and investors continued to bid up
stock prices. Speculating investors used small amounts of their
own cash and borrowed up to 70 or 80 percent of the purchase
price. This allowed them to buy shares of a stock, wait for the
stock's price to rise, sell the stock, repay the margin borrowing
with interest, and reap significant capital gains on their small

cash investment. But margin lending alone cannot explain the stock market boom. There was already a long history of margin lending on stock exchanges, and margin requirements—the share of the purchase price paid in cash—were no lower in the late twenties than in the early twenties or in previous decades. In fact, in the fall of 1928 margin requirements began to rise, and borrowers were required to pay a larger share of the purchase price of the stocks.

The economic downturn that began in the early summer of 1929 reduced profit expectations and worked its way to Wall Street. On September 3, 1929, the Dow Jones index reached its peak of 381 and then unevenly declined to 320 on October 21. The stock market crashed the following week with record declines and record numbers of shares changing hands on Black Thursday, October 24, and Tragic Tuesday, October 29. The index continued to decline as brokers cleaned up accounts and sold the stocks of clients who could not raise additional margin. On November 13, 1929, the slide stopped when the Dow Jones index hit 198. Some recovery occurred in the following months, and the Dow Jones index reached 294 in April 1930. It again began falling and continued to fall into the summer of 1932 when the Great Depression was well under way.

INITIAL STAGES OF THE GREAT CONTRACTION

Following the stock market crash, President Hoover moved to cushion the shock. A believer in planning, Hoover had concluded that he would not allow wages to decline and unemployment to rise as had occurred in the depression in 1920–1921. Hoover described that event as a "liquidation" of labor, stocks, farmers, and real estate. He convened a series of White House conferences with leaders of industrial, construction, and public utility firms on November 18, 21, 22, and 27, 1929, to coordinate actions of business and government agencies to minimize the harmful effects of the contraction and to keep the contraction brief. His message to all these groups was similar. Wage rates must be maintained to support labor's purchasing power. Labor was not a commodity and should not be liquidated. If these firms finally found it necessary to reduce wage rates, they should not be reduced by any more than the reduction in the cost of living. Firms should do everything they could to maintain employment, and any work reductions should be spread across the entire labor force by reducing the workweek rather than by laying off workers. The firms should allow their profits rather than wages to fall. In addition, they were to maintain, if not expand, their investment in buildings and machinery. The leaders publicly agreed to this at the November meetings and at a larger conference in Washington on December 5.

To ensure such actions, at Hoover's urging the Chamber of Commerce set up the National Business Survey Conference to survey and obtain pledges from businesses that they would maintain wages and undertake new investment. A new division in the Commerce Department attempted to speed federal construction projects and obtain commitments for more construction from state and local authorities. In 1929 the federal government again recorded a budget surplus, as it had since the beginning of the 1920s. Despite the reduction of federal personal income tax rates, the government had also reduced the outstanding federal debt by 25 percent. The surplus in 1929 gave Hoover the opportunity to propose an additional temporary tax reduction to help boost the economy, and Congress agreed to reduce income tax rates by 1 percent for each bracket for one year. Legislators also voted to increase public works expenditures by $400 million while labor union leaders agreed not to strike or demand higher wages.

The problem of falling land values for farmers had eased by the late 1920s, but in the latter part of the decade world grain prices began falling. Congress had twice passed McNary-Haugan bills to stabilize and support grain prices, but Calvin Coolidge had vetoed both bills. By 1928 agricultural leaders were urging Congress to pass a tariff to help protect farmers from falling commodity prices in the United States and in world markets. By 1929 Congress, with Hoover's approval, was debating such a tariff. To show his support for farmers, Hoover proposed the establishment of a Federal Farm Board, which was created in June 1929 with the passage of the Agricultural Marketing Act. With $100 million from the Treasury, the Federal Farm Board was authorized to make low-interest loans for up to twenty years to farm cooperatives to help support and stabilize agricultural commodity prices. (Co-ops bought and stored commodities when prices were lower—thus boosting them—and sold out when prices rose.) The Federal Farm Board was also authorized to create corporations to purchase grain when prices were falling. In November $150 million was lent to wheat cooperatives to purchase wheat. A Farmer's National Grain Corporation was created and given $10 million to centralize the marketing of wheat and other grains. Although wheat prices initially held steady, by the summer of 1930 wheat and other grain prices were falling. Farmers, anticipating stable wheat prices, had already begun planting more wheat for 1930, which exacerbated the problem. The Federal Farm Board now began directly purchasing wheat surpluses, and Congress gave the agency an additional $100 million in the spring of 1930. The accumulating surplus purchases frightened investors, and prices continued to fall. Ultimately the Federal Farm Board and its affiliates began selling their inventories, depressing prices and worsening the depression in the agricultural sector.

The contraction intensified the demand for a tariff bill—industry after industry pleaded for additional protection. The resulting Hawley-Smoot tariff sharply raised duties on a massive list of items imported into the United States. Despite an open letter from 1,038 economists urging him not to sign it, Hoover in June 1930 approved the legislation. International trade was already beginning to contract because of the world-wide depression, and the tariff accelerated this contraction. The agricultural sector, which initiated the call for a more protective tariff, received little help from the bill because in the 1920s there had been few imports of important commodities such as wheat, oats, corn, rye, cotton, peanuts, and rice. The tariff bill was necessary, however, because if the Federal Farm Board and cooperatives had been able to stabilize grain prices at levels above world prices, the protective tariff would have discouraged imports of grain.

Hoover saw some hope that these actions might have the effect he wanted. The contraction seemed to lessen in the first half of 1930, and stock market prices actually rose from mid-November through May. But from June 1930 on it was apparent the contraction was continuing to accelerate. Incomes continued to decline as real Gross National Product per capita fell 10.8 percent between 1929 and 1930. The average rate of unemployment in 1929 was 3.2 percent; by 1930 it was 8.9 percent. In December 1930 estimates place the unemployment rate at around 14 percent. Prices also fell during 1930. Consumer prices declined 2.6 percent between 1929 and 1930 while wholesale prices fell a much larger 9.6 percent. In contrast to rising unemployment and falling prices and national income, money wage rates in the larger businesses remained almost constant for much of 1930 as firms kept their pledge to Hoover. Only in the last quarter of 1930 did some companies finally begin to reduce money wage rates. But declining price levels raised real wage rates. Firms responded to falling sales by laying off workers and, as a result, unemployment rates began rising, especially late in 1930.

In 1930 a drought hit the southern regions of the United

States in a belt stretching from Maryland through Arkansas. Cotton crops withered and died, and landlords ran out of money to help penniless tenant farmers. By the fall of 1930, hunger was a serious problem in drought-stricken areas. Hoover relied on the Red Cross to provide supplies to the needy, but the Red Cross did not have adequate supplies. On January 3, 1931, hungry tenant farmers who had no food and no income marched on England, Arkansas, demanding that stores provide food to carry them through the winter. Hasty negotiations between the Red Cross and local representatives led to the opening of a local grocery store and the distribution of provisions to the needy. The story of the march on England, Arkansas, was carried across the United States as an ominous sign of events. Similar "food riots" occurred in other cities that winter—Oklahoma City on January 20, Minneapolis on February 25, and later in San Francisco and St. Louis.

The next indication that something different was happening came in November and December 1930 when many banks in the southeastern United States failed. Most of these, like bank failures in earlier months, were small banks in agricultural areas where ill-considered loans and investments in the 1920s had left the banks in poor financial condition. Declining crop prices at the end of the 1920s and in the initial stages of the depression made it difficult for farmers and merchants to repay their loans. But there was more to the problem than this. Most of the banks failed in the last two weeks of November and then, in another spurt, in December. They were related to the failure of Caldwell and Company in Nashville, Tennessee, the largest investment banking house in the South. To help float and place new bond issues, Caldwell had established the Bank of Tennessee and gained control of several bank chains and the largest insurance group in the Southeast. By the late 1920s Caldwell was experiencing financial problems because of inadequate cash and liquid assets; in June 1930 it merged with the Banco Kentucky holding company. But Banco Kentucky was itself in financial difficulty and expected Caldwell to bail them out.

When Caldwell failed in November, its complex structure tumbled down like a house of cards. In Little Rock, Arkansas, the collapse led to the failure of the Caldwell-controlled American Exchange Trust, because that summer the bank had lent the Caldwell-controlled Home Insurance Company $100,000. With the disclosure of the failure of this major borrower, a run developed and the American Exchange Trust lost $4 million of $15 million in deposits in four days. In chain banking, the key bank holds most of the reserves for the other banks; within days forty-five other banks in the Arkansas chain failed. That failure brought down the Banco Kentucky, and fifteen Kentucky banks associated with it now failed. Down went ten more banks in Tennessee and fifteen banks in western Carolina with ties to Caldwell and the Bank of Tennessee. A smaller flurry of bank failures in the same region occurred in December, because of ties to the failed Caldwell and Company.

In December 1930 the Brooklyn, New York, Bank of the United States failed. At the start of the 1920s this had been a small bank serving a largely Jewish population in Brooklyn. The son of the founder rapidly expanded it, and by the end of the decade the bank's large real estate portfolio made its position shaky. When the bank failed, it was the largest single bank failure to date. As banks weakened around the United States during 1930 and 1931 because of the continuing contraction, more banks began to fail and conditions continued to deteriorate. Americans who worried about the safety of the banks began systematically to reduce their bank deposits in favor of holding more cash.

THE COLLAPSING WORLD ECONOMY, 1931

The depression was not confined to the United States; it was worldwide. Germany had been in a slump since 1928, and the contraction began in 1929 for many other countries. By 1930 the depression was affecting all the developed countries. The downturn was especially severe in Central Europe, where countries had experienced difficult adjustments after the breakup of the Austro-Hungarian Empire at the end of Word War I. Austria had been the region's financial center, and Austrian banks had close ties to the industries and firms they financed. But the breakup had severed these ties. As in Germany and Britain, unemployment in Austria had remained high and growth slow throughout the 1920s. The early twenties inflation, though not as severe as the hyperinflation in Germany, had reduced the capital of banks and left them in a weakened position. In the late twenties, mergers, often between relatively weak banks, had sharply reduced the number of banks in Austria. One large bank, the Bodenkreditanstalt, had taken over several banks in the late twenties, and in 1929 it was merged into the Credit-Anstalt. The Bodenkreditanstalt brought to the merger a great many slow industrial loans and accumulated losses that exceeded its capital. The Credit-Anstalt, which was now larger than all the other banks in Austria combined, had its own problems well before the merger. The merger magnified the bank's difficulties.

An accountant's report released in early May 1930 revealed the losses and disturbing financial condition of the Credit-Anstalt. The government, the Austrian National Bank, and the House of Rothschild provided loans to the bank to help support it. But as the public learned of its weakness, runs on the bank by Austrian and foreign depositors began. Countries at this time were on a gold standard with a fixed exchange rate, and were obligated to exchange gold for their currencies when asked to do so. Foreign and domestic depositors converted their deposits into currency and then asked the Austrian government to exchange gold for their shillings. As the government's gold reserves began to fall precipitously, several international loans were arranged to provide the government with additional reserves. These were too late and too small, and the crisis worsened. By late June, strict controls on foreign exchange were imposed to halt the flow of gold out of Austria. Domestic depositors were strongly discouraged from converting deposits into gold and foreign exchange, and Austria effectively left the gold standard.

By the end of May 1931 the Austrian crisis was spreading into neighboring Central European countries. Panicky domestic and foreign depositors began runs on banks in Poland, Czechoslovakia, Romania, Hungary, and Germany. The Credit-Anstalt held a controlling interest in the largest bank in Budapest, and its troubles overflowed to that and other Hungarian banks. By August, Hungary too had imposed strict controls on foreign exchange and had effectively left the gold standard. But Germany was the largest and most important of these countries. German banks had relatively low levels of reserves that could be paid to depositors, as most of their assets were tied up in loans. Economic activity in Germany began declining in 1928. During the last half of the 1920s, Germany had been a major recipient of foreign loans and deposits, and by 1930 more than half the deposits in German banks were foreign. The flow of loans and deposits from the United States, which helped to make reparations payments, had declined sharply in 1928 and 1929 as funds were diverted into the booming American stock market. The result was that most of the assets of German banks were tied up in relatively illiquid loans to poorly performing firms. When Austria imposed foreign exchange controls, freezing foreign deposits in

Austrian banks, foreign investors turned to German banks where deposits were not frozen—yet. Fearing that Germany would do the same, foreign investors began to convert deposits into currency and currency into gold to withdraw from the country. Thus Germany's gold reserves too began to decline.

The failure of a large woolen firm, Nordwoole, led to large losses at its bank, the Danatbank. Withdrawals from the Danatbank and the large Berlin banks accelerated as confidence in German banks waned. The German government continued to lose gold to the point where further losses would force it off the gold standard. Germany froze foreign deposits in German banks and placed strict controls on foreign exchange to allow the Reichsbank to control foreign transactions. Germany, like Austria and Hungary, had effectively left the gold standard.

Britain was the next country to come under fire. It had experienced difficulties throughout the 1920s with higher rates of unemployment and slower rates of growth than other countries. Britain consistently imported more goods than it exported, but this "trade deficit" was balanced by a surplus in earnings from services—tourism, shipping on British vessels, and financial services provided for foreigners—and from interest, profits, and dividends from British overseas investments. By 1931 all these payments were declining as international trade shrank and the worldwide depression reduced commercial activity and profits. Many British-held South American loans had already gone into default. During the 1920s the British pound had been, together with the American dollar, a key international reserve for many countries who held significant amounts of their international reserves in pounds and dollars rather than gold. Consequently foreign governments held a large amount of British pounds.

The reduction in "invisible" earnings had weakened the

pound by the time of the crisis in Central Europe. With Germany, Austria, and Hungary freezing foreign deposits, smaller European countries, most notably Sweden, Belgium, the Netherlands, and Switzerland, turned to Britain for liquidity and began to redeem pounds for gold. Appeals for temporary loans from the United States and France were unsuccessful. New German bankruptcies accelerated the conversion of foreign-held pounds into gold, and on September 21, 1931, Great Britain officially abandoned the gold standard. The pound immediately began to depreciate. Now only the United States dollar remained as a key international reserve currency for the nations of the world.

The crisis of a collapsing gold standard now shifted to Washington. Worried that the United States might behave like Britain and Germany, the central banks of France, the Netherlands, Belgium, and Switzerland began liquidating dollars for American gold. Although the United States tried to reassure the central bankers and foreign dollar holders that it would remain on the gold standard, the loss of gold through dollar liquidation continued. On October 9, 1931, the Federal Reserve System, the United States' central bank, raised interest rates from 1.5 to 2.5 percent. One week later it raised interest rates from 2.5 to 3.5 percent. By September and October 1931 prices were falling about 1 percent a month. Even if interest rates had been zero, those who held money would have received a 1 percent per month return due to the falling prices. But the Federal Reserve's actions had sharply increased real interest rates in the United States. The interest rate increases drove existing financial securities' prices down as their yields rose. Because foreign investors had to sell U.S. securities to obtain dollars for conversion into gold, the decline in securities' prices and rise in their yields made it more costly to sell U.S. assets. The interest rate increases halted the conversion of dollars into gold, and by November 1931 there was, in fact, a small flow of gold back into the United States to buy dollars to purchase American securities.

These actions accelerated the contraction in the United States. American bank failures had risen after the Austrian and German banking crises. Losses on bank loans increased, and banks that held foreign securities saw the value of those securities fall, causing bank assets to fall and forcing some banks into bankruptcy. Failures again rose sharply after Britain's departure from gold, and the interest rate increases in the United States brought on more losses and more declines in the value of bank assets. Economic activity contracted much more rapidly in late 1931 and early 1932, and unemployment rates rose from 15 percent in June to 16.7 percent in October to nearly 20 percent in December 1931. The worldwide depression had led to a dramatic reduction in international trade. Total imports of seventy-five leading nations fell from about $3 billion in October 1929 to $1.4 billion in December 1931 and finally to less than $1 billion in July 1932. By the end of 1932 only the United States, France, Belgium, the Netherlands, and Switzerland remained fully on the gold standard. Other nations had either officially abandoned it or effectively abandoned it by imposing strict controls on foreign exchange and foreign transactions.

CONTINUING DECLINE, INCREASING UNREST, AND THE FINAL BANKING PANIC, 1932–1933

Bank failures in the United States rose rapidly in the last quarter of 1931. The pace of economic contraction slowed in the first quarter of 1932, but by May unemployment again began increasing. From a 23.7 percent unemployment rate in May, the rate reached 27.9 percent by September and then declined to 22.3 percent in December. In most European countries the contraction ended in 1931, but in the United States it continued on into 1932 and 1933. On Wall Street, the decline in stock market prices bottomed out in the summer of 1932 and then began slowly to rise.

By this time calls for government action were coming from many conflicting quarters. Hoover called "economy conferences" to try to explain what his administration viewed as desirable cutbacks in government spending. His administration also proposed, and Congress passed, the Revenue Act of 1932 in an attempt to reduce the growing federal budget deficit. This act resulted in massive increases in taxes. Normal federal personal income tax rates were doubled, and the surtax rates were raised dramatically. The top surtax rate—on personal income above $750,000—was increased from 25 to 63 percent. Wartime excise taxes were revived, other taxes increased, and new taxes proposed. Taxes were imposed on the sale of gasoline, tires, autos, electric energy, malt, toiletries, furs, jewelry, and other articles. Taxes on admissions to theaters and movies and on stock transfers increased. The act levied new taxes on bank checks, bond transfers, telephone, telegraph, and radio messages.

Faithful to his concept of cooperation between the public and private spheres, Hoover proposed new cooperation to stem the decline in the economy. At Hoover's urging, Congress approved the Reconstruction Finance Corporation to invest in and lend to the banks in an attempt to stabilize the banking system. The Glass-Steagall Act authorized the Federal Reserve System to use federal government bonds as backing for the money it created; the Farm Loan Board was given expanded powers to aid the farming sector; and a new federal discount bank to back home mortgages was authorized. Hoover proposed a significant restriction in immigration as a means of reducing unemployment and making work for American citizens, and he wanted to reform the bankruptcy laws to weaken protection for creditors of bankrupt enterprises.

Popular frustration with the seemingly unending depression now began to surface. By the end of 1931 the dramatic decline in the sales of Ford cars led to massive layoffs and cuts in Ford wage rates, from $7 to $6 and finally to $4 a day. Ford produced 1,436,000 cars in 1929, but by 1932 production had declined to about 400,000 cars and the giant River Rouge plant was, at times, as quiet as a tomb. Henry Ford and his internal police, managed by Harry Bennett, were viewed with distrust by the people of Detroit. On a cold March 7, 1932, Communist organizers and the Detroit Unemployed Council led 3,000 men and women on a hunger march toward Gate 3 at the Rouge plant in Dearborn, Michigan. As soon as they crossed the city line from Detroit to Dearborn, the Dearborn police and Ford security police ordered them to turn back to Detroit. When the marchers ignored the directives, the police waded in with tear gas and nightsticks. Gunfire soon erupted, and by the end of the battle 4 marchers were dead and 60 wounded. The police then arrested all the radicals they could find.

In May 1932, Des Moines, Iowa, hosted the convention of the National Farmers' Union. The NFU's president, Milo Reno, was convinced that farmers' only recourse to low farm prices was to strike—by withholding their output from the market. Reno, who had initially studied for the ministry and whose fiery oratory led the NFU, had advocated a strike or boycott since 1927. He argued that if farmers withheld their livestock and produce, especially milk, from market, prices would rise to the point where farmers could again earn an income that at least covered their costs of production. The NFU convention authorized a Farmer's Holiday Association to persuade farmers to withhold sales. The strike began in August as farmers blockaded roads and sometimes forcibly turned

back trucks carrying produce to markets. The action was centered in Iowa, Minnesota, and Wisconsin, but some strike activities were also seen in neighboring states. Although strikers
were sometimes arrested and, under pressure from farmers,
released from jail, the strike never won significant support
among farmers.

Milo Reno and the National Farmers' Union also encouraged farmers to rebel at farm foreclosure sales. In late 1932
and 1933 farmers attempted to forcibly stop evictions and
break up such sales. In other cases they banded together to bid
on properties at very low prices. One study estimated that at
least seventy-six foreclosure sales were blocked by these methods in January and February 1933. Agricultural interests pur-
sued a moratorium on farm mortgage foreclosures. Iowa
legislators got the message and on February 17, 1933, passed a
mortgage foreclosure moratorium law. On February 25, 1933,
Minnesota Governor Floyd Olson issued a decree establishing
a one-year moratorium on farm mortgage foreclosures; other
farm states passed similar laws. The Supreme Court upheld
the constitutionality of these moratoriums despite the Fifth
Amendment's protection against the taking of private property—in this case, that of the mortgage holders.

The largest expression of discontent was the Bonus Army's
1932 march on Washington. In 1924, Congress had passed a
bonus bill for veterans of World War I. Money was to be
placed in an endowment fund to earn interest, so that in 1945
each veteran would receive an average of $1,000. The Ameri-
can Legion had pushed the bill for four years, and Congress
had overridden President Calvin Coolidge's veto to enact it. In
February 1931, Congress overrode Hoover's veto and passed
the Emergency Adjusted Compensation Act. It allowed the
veterans to borrow, at low interest rates, about half the money
they had been scheduled to receive in 1945. By 1932 demands
for the outright payment of the bonus were growing. In early

May the House Ways and Means Committee recommended against a bill proposing this. Walter Waters, an unemployed veteran in Portland, Oregon, then began a march of unemployed veterans from Portland to Washington, D.C., to demand payment of the bonus. Picking up fresh recruits along the way, the "Bonus Expeditionary Army" reached Washington at the end of May. Within weeks they were joined by thousands more marchers. It was estimated that, at the peak of the protest, perhaps 25,000 marchers were living in 27 encampments around Washington. Inspired by the presence of the marchers, the House of Representatives suddenly resurrected and passed the bonus bill. But on June 17 the Senate defeated it, and marchers gradually began to drift back home.

On July 9, President Hoover signed a bill to give marchers money to return to their homes. As the bill's deadline of July 24 came and passed, eight thousand to ten thousand veterans remained in Washington. With the passing of the deadline and Bonus Army marchers still encamped in the city, Hoover decided it was time to remove them from downtown Washington. On July 27 he issued orders to Pelham Glassford, chief of police in the District of Columbia, to do this. In the afternoon of July 28, Glassford and the police confronted the unemployed veterans at the Anacostia Bridge. Hoover was asked to send in troops to assist the police. Although General Douglas MacArthur had orders to cooperate with the police and use as little force as possible, he cleared the buildings in Washington, drove the Bonus Army back to the Anacostia Bridge, and then burned all of the marchers' makeshift huts on Anacostia Flats. The fires could be seen for miles as the Bonus Army marchers began straggling out of Washington. Hoover took all the blame for the incident, never mentioning that MacArthur had directly disobeyed his orders. From that moment on, Hoover's reelection campaign was doomed.

By late summer 1932 there were signs of improved business

activity and perhaps the end of the depression. Hoover tried to make the most of these signs in his fall reelection campaign against Franklin D. Roosevelt, but the economy faltered and the bitter presidential election campaign increased Americans' anxiety. In July 1932, Congress required that the Reconstruction Finance Corporation report the names of all banks that were borrowing from the RFC. House Speaker John Nance Garner then began weekly releases of this list of banks. Borrowing by banks to strengthen their capital began to decline, and there is some evidence that the publication of the names of borrowing banks increased depositor withdrawals and, in some cases, bank failures. Although the bank failure rate was lower in 1932 than in 1931, that rate began to increase at the end of the year.

The presidential election gave Roosevelt a landslide victory and swept a Democratic-dominated Senate and House into power. After the election, rumors began circulating that Roosevelt would devalue the dollar relative to gold in an attempt to stimulate recovery. The president-elect refused to confirm or deny the rumors and would say nothing about his planned economic policies. He sought to distance himself from Hoover's failed programs. Critics contend that he was also allowing the economy to contract so that he would look more like a savior when he took office and began his own efforts. Thus in January and February, Hoover was handcuffed in his attempts to propose policies that might reverse the declining economy.

In October 1932, just before Election day, an important chain of banks in Nevada had appeared on the verge of failure. With few banks in the state, Nevada authorities were worried about the effects of a failure of a significant portion of the state's banks. On October 31, 1932, they took the dramatic step of declaring a bank holiday—first in the nation—to relieve the banks of the necessity of meeting withdrawal demands from depositors. Nevada's action began to spread liquidity pressure to banks in other states and offered an example for other states to follow.

In January 1933 the House of Representatives released the names of all the banks that had received RFC loans before August 1932. This increased the conversion of deposits to currency, further weakening the banks. New demands also appeared. Some depositors specifically began requesting gold, not just currency. If Roosevelt did decide to devalue the dollar, each ounce of gold would suddenly be worth more dollars than before, and each dollar of currency would be worth less gold than before. Clearly those who held gold would gain from a devaluation. As Roosevelt continued to refuse to comment on his economic plans, the runs on banks grew, economic contraction accelerated, and unemployment levels increased.

Banks simply did not have enough cash or gold reserves to convert all or most of their deposits. The Federal Reserve System, the nation's central bank, was unable or unwilling to provide either. As banks tried to sell loans and securities (where they could find buyers) to obtain cash to pay panicky depositors, the prices of the loans and securities declined and the bank's assets fell to less than their liabilities—bankruptcy. Thus bank runs and failures rose during the period between Roosevelt's election and his swearing in as President in March 1933. The state of Iowa declared a bank holiday in January. It was followed by Louisiana and Michigan in early February. In late February, Maryland, Arkansas, Indiana, and Ohio declared bank holidays to restrict withdrawals from banks. Banks still open and trying to meet withdrawal demands were reducing their account balances at the large New York City and Chicago banks where the nation's financial markets were centered. Bank holidays relieved the pressure on the banks in those states where the holiday was imposed, but this merely shifted the withdrawal pressure to banks in nearby states that were still open. Hoover worked tirelessly to prevent bank holidays right up to Roosevelt's inauguration. Realizing that the closing of banks in New York and Chicago would signal the shutdown of the entire system, he sent urgent pleas to the governors of New York and Illinois to persevere. On Saturday morning, March 4, 1933, however, both governors capitulated and declared bank holidays in their states. By that time thirty states had declared bank holidays, and where banks remained open, restrictions on withdrawals were often imposed. In many cities, scrip was issued because of the shortage of cash as banks closed.

THE STATE OF THE ECONOMY IN MARCH 1933

The collapsing financial system led to a further contraction of economic activity. By March 1933 more than 28 percent of the labor force was unemployed. Excluding the agricultural sector, the unemployment rate may have approached 38 percent. Unemployment varied by region. In the South Atlantic states, for example, employment fell less and recovered more quickly after 1933, even surpassing its pre-1929 levels. The areas that suffered the heaviest unemployment were the major industrial areas of the East North Central and mid-Atlantic regions, because of the dramatic decline in production in the heavy industries, and the mountain region where much mining was located. Durable manufacturing—which includes such items as steel and other metals, automobiles, trucks, farm implements, tires, large household appliances, and business machinery and equipment—in March 1933 was only 23 percent of the volume achieved in July 1929. In contrast, nondurable manufacturing—for example, clothes, books, processed food, and household utensils—in March 1933 was at 70 percent of the volume of June 1929.

The purchases of durable goods can be much more easily postponed; such goods can be repaired or reconditioned and continue to provide services. As depression-era consumers took this approach, the demand and production of durable goods and capital goods for business investment plummeted. And the combination of reduced spending and falling prices led to increased rates of business failure. During the 1920s the annual business failure rate had averaged about 100 per 10,000 enterprises. By 1932 this failure rate had increased more than 50 percent.

The financial system had been devastated during the long contraction. In 1929 there were 24,970 commercial banks in the United States; in 1933 there were 14,207. The largest banks, most of which had national charters, were members of the Federal Reserve System, and the number of these banks fell from 8,707 in 1929 to 5,606 in 1933 as 27.5 percent of the member banks failed. Much more numerous were the small independent banks that had state charters and were not members of the Federal Reserve. These banks dominated banking in the rural areas, small towns, cities, and suburbs of the largest cities. There were 16,263 nonmember banks in 1929 but only 8,601 in 1933. Between 1929 and 1933 more than 45 percent of all small nonmember banks failed.

The failure of a bank had dreadful consequences for its community. The federal government insured none of the deposits in banks before 1933, and the few state attempts at deposit insurance could not withstand major contractions such as the Great Depression. Most families and individuals used banks to hold their savings in savings accounts and time deposits. Most businesses and wealthier families and individuals held checking account deposits. When a bank entered bankruptcy, all activities and account transactions were suspended. The bankruptcy judge would begin selling the bank's assets, such as loans, securities, and real property, in order to obtain funds to pay the bank's creditors. This process generally took several years, frequently longer, and during this interval depositors could not convert any of their accounts in the failed bank into money. If they were lucky, when the liquidation was complete they might receive most of the funds they had on deposit at the time of the failure, but often they received less, say, sixty or seventy cents for each dollar of deposits. Businesses that had relied on the bank for lines of credit and other business loans were forced to turn elsewhere, if such sources of borrowed funds could be found at all. And business deposits in the failed bank were frozen just like the deposits of families and individuals. As a consequence, both families and businesses in the failed bank's area lost part of their wealth, and they reduced household and investment spending accordingly. Between 1929 and 1933 there were 9,765 bank failures in the United States.

2

What Caused the Great Depression?

THE GREAT DEPRESSION of the early 1930s stands out as one of the most important events of the twentieth century. It was very severe in the United States and Germany but, in varying degrees, less so in Canada, France, Britain, Eastern Europe, and the Scandinavian countries. The rise to power of Hitler and the Nazi party in Germany was the result of the depression there. It was shorter in Japan and Britain but longer in France. Central and South American and other Asian countries also experienced economic contraction. Explaining why it occurred and why it was so severe in America requires a theoretical framework to show how the forces that brought on the depression worked and why they existed.

MARKETS, PRICES, AND ECONOMIC CONTRACTIONS

A decentralized market economy is an amazing institution. Hundreds of thousands of producers hire millions of workers, purchase uncounted amounts of raw materials and manufactured inputs from hundreds of thousands of other producers, and use these to produce millions of products and services which are then distributed to all parts of an economy, such as the United States, to sell to consumers whom the producers have never met and do not know. This takes place con-

tinuously, with constant adjustments to the changing demands of consumers, the changing availability of various resources, changes in technology, and the introduction of new
commodities and services. Normally most all of the workers
who want a job are employed, and the owners of buildings,
machinery, land, and mines find a use for the resources they
own. Sometimes, however, this rhythm of ongoing economic
activity is interrupted, and the economy becomes depressed.
Production falls and the employment and incomes of workers
and of nonhuman resources declines, though not all industries
are affected to the same extent.

Workers do not "disappear"—they are unemployed. Buildings, machinery, trucks, railroads, mines, and farmland are
not destroyed—many of these resources simply sit idle and
unused during a depression. The knowledge of how to employ resources to manufacture products and provide services is
not lost—it is simply not put to use.

A market economy uses prices as the primary device to coordinate the economic activities that take place in a society—
the purchasing and producing of commodities and services.
Millions of consumers choose from hundreds of thousands of
different commodities and services. Producers choose from
thousands of different resources and methods in producing
these commodities and services and in choosing how much to
produce. Rather than a central director or committee determining the allocation of resources and the levels of production, a decentralized market system uses market-determined
prices. Consumers decide what and how much of different
products and services to purchase based on their incomes, the
prices of what they want, and their preferences for different
products and services. Consumers' decisions on purchases provide the revenues by which producers demand the resources
necessary to produce those commodities and services. Payments to the owners of the resources provide the incomes with

which they can go to the markets and, as consumers, demand various commodities and services. This system of relative prices coordinates all of the activities.

As an example, if consumers demand more beef they will purchase more of it and less of other meat. Prices for beef will rise, and the prices of competing meats will fall. In response, ranchers and farmers will begin producing more beef and less pork, poultry, and other types of meat. They reallocate resources away from the production of competing meats to the production of beef, consistent with the change in consumer tastes. Meat packers will begin shipping more beef to supermarkets as consumers have demanded. In general, if some markets have an excess demand (the quantity demanded exceeds the quantity supplied at the current price), other markets will have an excess supply (the quantity demanded is less than the quantity supplied at the current price). Shifting prices will lead resource owners to move away from markets with excess supply toward markets with excess demand, and consumers to shift some of their purchases toward markets where there is excess supply. In this way the excess demands and excess supplies are eliminated. All of these changes occur because of changes in relative prices. Millions of such relative price adjustments take place constantly, all working to allocate scarce resources to producing those goods and services on which consumers place the highest value.

Money prices are a kind of low-cost information that makes possible specialization and exchange through a division of labor while coordinating demands and production. Costly information and movement through space make perfect coordination impossible, but market systems generally work well and adjust to changes in consumer demands and changes in the supply of various resources. In a free market system at its best, unemployment is minimized.

A depression occurs when something disrupts this process

so that resource owners and consumers cannot accurately identify and respond to change. Because money prices are the primary coordinating agents in a market economy, the price system may be disrupted by disturbances to the monetary system. A pronounced decline in the money supply will cause prices to fall (less money available to purchase all that's produced), but not all prices will fall simultaneously. This is the most common cause of depressions.

To understand the nature of the worldwide Great Depression and the severity and greater length of the American contraction, one must therefore understand something about the nature and characteristics of money. Three essential features are banks and the creation and destruction of money; the role of the Federal Reserve System in creating and destroying money; and the gold standard and fixed exchange rates.

BANKS AND THE CREATION AND DESTRUCTION OF MONEY

Gold coins, other minor copper and silver coins, and the paper currency that is held by the public (excluding the banks) are part of the money supply, but the demand deposits (or checking accounts) that banks create for the public are the most important part. Banks are in the business of borrowing from depositors and lending to borrowers through the creation of demand deposits. A bank will lend what would otherwise be idle balances from depositors' accounts by creating (or adding to) a demand deposit for the borrower. The borrower can then write a check to spend the borrowed funds. Demand deposits are part of the money supply because a depositor, by signing a check, can authorize the bank to pay a portion of the depositor's demand deposit to the bearer of that check. Thus purchases can be directly made by writing checks on the demand deposit.

There is, however, a crucial difference between demand deposits and other types of money. By the late nineteenth century banks operated on the principle of "fractional reserve" banking. Banks continuously debit demand deposits as checks clear, and credit demand deposits as customers make deposits. Most of the time, currency paid out as checks are cleared is approximately offset by currency received for new deposits. It is unlikely that all or many of the depositors will simultaneously attempt to convert their demand deposits into gold or currency (which was also backed by gold). Under "fractional reserve" banking, banks keep only a fraction of their deposit liabilities in gold or currency reserves. The rest of the reserves backing up the deposits are loaned to borrowers to generate the income to pay the bank's expenses, provide dividends for the bank's stockholders, and pay interest to the depositors.

An example will show how the banking system can create (and destroy) money through fractional reserve banking. Suppose that a gold miner in Lead, South Dakota, mined 242 ounces of gold (about $5,000). The Denver mint would strike $5,000 in gold coins from this supply of new gold. Then, because it was safer and more convenient, the miner would deposit the $5,000 in gold coins in his demand deposit in the Cattlemen's Bank in Denver. By the late nineteenth century, federal laws required banks with a national charter to hold a minimum percentage of their deposits in cash reserves composed of gold (and silver) coins and currency (national banknotes). Most states had similar reserve requirements for state-chartered banks. The Denver bank would have been required to hold 12.5 percent of its deposits in cash reserves and might have kept some excess reserves as a precaution against unexpected deposit withdrawals. Assuming that it normally held 15 percent of its deposits in gold and currency, it would want to keep $750 of this new deposit in reserves. The rest could be lent to borrowers to generate income.

As borrowers obtained loans, the bank would lend them money by creating a new demand deposit for the borrower or adding to the borrower's current demand deposit. Once the bank had made loans equaling all of its new excess reserves of $4,250, it could make no additional loans until it obtained additional excess reserves through new deposits or current loans being paid off. But the story does not end here. The firm that borrowed the $4,250 would spend that amount. The firm receiving the check for $4,250 would then deposit the check in its bank, say the First National Bank of Denver. The First National Bank would send the check to the Cattlemen's Bank where $4,250 would be deducted from the borrowing firm's deposit and $4,250 would be sent to the First National Bank. The Cattlemen's Bank would then have no remaining excess reserves for loans from the miner's $5,000 deposit.

But the First National Bank now would have a new demand deposit for $4,250 and new cash reserves of $4,250, but at 15 percent it would hold only $637.50 in reserves against this new deposit. The First National Bank would lend out its new excess reserves of $3,612.50 by creating (or adding to) a demand deposit for a borrower. When this second borrower spent the $3,612.50 and the check cleared at the First National Bank, this bank would also have no excess reserves for loans. But the $3,612.50 check would be deposited in a demand deposit in another bank, say the Second National Bank of Colorado Springs, Colorado. The Second National Bank would now have excess reserves of $3,070.63 and would lend this out by creating (or adding to) a demand deposit for a borrower.

Consider what has happened thus far. A miner has dug up $5,000 worth of gold and, after having it struck into coins, deposited it in the Cattlemen's Bank. The new $5,000 of gold has been converted into a new demand deposit of $5,000. The money supply has increased by $5,000. Because banks keep only a fraction of their deposits in reserves, the Cattlemen's

Bank lent the excess reserves, and these became a new demand deposit of $4,250 in the First National Bank. The First National Bank then had excess reserves, which became a new demand deposit of $3,612.50 in the Second National Bank. The new reserves of $5,000 (the gold the miner found) have increased the demand deposit money by $12,862.50, and the process is not finished because the Second National Bank now has excess reserves to lend out. This process of expanding the money supply through the creation of demand deposits would continue until all of the $5,000 in gold ended up as required and precautionary reserves backing up demand deposits, potentially increasing the money supply by $33,333. Because of the leverage created by fractional reserve banking, relatively small changes in reserves can create much larger changes in the money supply.

An example will illustrate the problems that may arise with fractional reserve banking. On October 14, 1907, five banks in New York City experienced difficulty as a larger than normal number of their depositors began converting deposits into currency. On October 21, 1907, New York's Knickerbocker Trust Company experienced runs on its deposits and failed. On October 24 panicky depositors at the second largest trust company in the city began a run on its deposits. Worried depositors at other banks begin converting deposits into cash, mainly currency. Concerned banks outside New York with deposits in New York banks now began converting those deposits to currency and gold. Depositors at banks in other Eastern cities, seeing the panic in New York banks, began converting deposits at their banks into currency. By late October 1907 a nationwide banking panic had developed. Under a fractional reserve banking system, the banks could not pay out cash to large numbers of their depositors because the bulk of the deposits were held in income-earning securities, not currency and gold. Banks had nowhere to turn to obtain additional cash easily. If large numbers of banks entered the open market to sell these securities in order to obtain cash to pay panicky depositors, this would drive down the price of the securities; the banks might not have sufficient assets to cover their liabilities and thus would be bankrupt. Banks thus began suspending or restricting the redemption of deposits into currency and gold. But they continued to clear checks and make loans, and borrowers continued to make payments on loans. This ended the panic, as it had done in previous banking panics, but as a safety precaution banks increased the percentage of their deposits they kept as cash reserves. And depositors, for a while, held somewhat more currency and less demand deposits.

To build up reserves, that is, increase the percentage of deposits held as reserves from 15 to 20 percent, banks would reduce their lending. For example, if borrowers paid back $100,000 on current loans, the banks might create only $85,000 in new loans. They could do this by increasing the interest rates charged on loans and thus reducing loan demand. The demand deposits destroyed by paying back the loans was larger than the demand deposits created by new loans. Increasing the reserve ratio (or percentage of deposits held as cash reserves) thus reduced the money supply. For example, the miner's new $5,000 in gold would result in $25,000 in new demand deposits at a 20 percent reserve ratio as opposed to $33,333 at a 15 percent reserve ratio. In addition, at a 20 percent ratio each dollar that a depositor converted into currency, rather than holding it in a demand deposit, would require that the banking system destroy $5 in demand deposits. At a 15 percent reserve ratio each dollar of demand deposits converted into cash required the destruction of $6.67 of demand deposits.

With fractional reserve banking, relatively small changes in reserves were multiplied into much larger changes in the money supply. In 1907 banks responded to the October runs by building up their excess reserves. The money supply shrank, and the reduction in spending led to more rapidly falling prices. This transformed a relatively minor economic contraction into a rapid and severe decline in economic activity that did not end until June 1908.

Banks acted as lenders to business firms and individuals in the United States, but there was no "bank" to lend to the banks—there was no "lender of last resort," or bankers' bank, in the United States that could make loans to the banks themselves when banks required additional currency. And by the early twentieth century there began to be a need for such an institution.

THE FEDERAL RESERVE SYSTEM

Congress created the Federal Reserve System in 1913, and in November 1914 it opened its doors for business. The Federal Reserve Banks were to furnish an elastic currency for the United States, afford a means of discounting commercial paper for the nation's commercial banks (i.e., buying up IOUs received by banks for their loans), and provide a better means of supervising the nation's banks. Congress worried about creating a monopoly by authorizing one great Federal Reserve Bank, so it created twelve banks serving regional districts—in Boston, New York City, Philadelphia, Richmond, Atlanta, Cleveland, Chicago, Minneapolis, Kansas City, St. Louis, Dallas, and San Francisco. Their activities were to be coordinated by a Federal Reserve Board in Washington, D.C., but the responsibilities of the Board were not clearly spelled out in the original act.

The Federal Reserve Banks were expected to become bankers for the nation's banks. When banks needed additional cash reserves to pay to panicky depositors, the Federal Reserve Banks were to provide these cash reserves. The bank would use short-term commercial paper as security for the loan from the Federal Reserve Bank (this was called "discounting"). Short-term commercial paper–IOUs for loans to businesses with a maturity of less than one year–was considered "self-liquidating" and relatively safe. To make these loans the Federal Reserve Banks were authorized to print currency (Federal Reserve Notes) and give this to the borrowing bank. The currency was backed by gold and the commercial paper submitted by the borrowing banks. Commercial banks that were members of the Federal Reserve System were also required to hold their reserves against deposits as accounts at their regional Federal Reserve Bank, which could then simply credit the borrowing bank's reserve account. The Federal Reserve Banks could control the amount of bank borrowing by varying the discount rate, or the rate at which commercial banks borrowed from the Federal Reserve System.

This system was expected to end bank panics by providing the liquidity that banks had to have. If a panic occurred, the bank simply borrowed from the Federal Reserve Bank using its commercial paper (its loans to businesses) as security, and paid the Federal Reserve Notes to panicky depositors. It was anticipated that when depositors saw that the bank was capable of converting deposits into currency as they demanded, the panic would end. The commercial banks' deposits of reserves at Federal Reserve Banks were also working deposits. Checks would be cleared within regions and across the country by debiting and crediting the reserve accounts of member banks rather than waiting as a check made its way toward the bank on which it was drawn.

Federal Reserve Banks were to have enough gold to back up 35 percent of the reserve deposits of member commercial banks and 40 percent of the Federal Reserve Notes outstanding. They were to have enough additional gold or eligible securities to back up the remaining 60 percent of the outstanding Federal Reserve Notes. Federal Reserve Banks were to generate the income to cover their operating costs and pay interest to their stockholders (the member commercial banks who were required to buy stock in the system) through discounting for their member banks. If discounting proved inadequate, the Federal Reserve Banks were authorized to enter the open market and buy commercial paper and government securities on their own account to earn income. By the mid-1920s the Federal Reserve Banks realized that when they did this they affected the reserves of the banks and thus the money supply. The banks then began coordinating these open-market operations, and all transactions for the regional banks were centralized at the New York Federal Reserve Bank.

Although a Federal Reserve Bank could print currency with which to buy securities in the open market, ordinarily it simply wrote a check on the bank. For example, suppose that the Chicago Federal Reserve Bank purchased $100,000 worth of commercial paper on the open market, and that the seller was a commercial paper broker with a demand deposit account at a bank in Peoria, Illinois. The seller would deposit the check in his account at the Peoria bank, which would send the check to the Chicago Federal Reserve Bank to credit to the Peoria bank's reserve account. The Peoria bank now had an additional $100,000 in a demand deposit and an additional $100,000 in reserves. With a reserve requirement for city banks of 10 percent, the Peoria bank needed only $10,000 in reserves and therefore had $90,000 in excess reserves. It would lend out these new reserves, and through the fractional reserve banking system the stock of money would begin to grow. The Federal Reserve System could control the reserves of the banks by lending through the discount window or by buying and selling commercial paper and government securities through the open market. And thus the system could control the money supply as well as be a lender of last resort to halt banking panics.

THE GOLD STANDARD, FIXED EXCHANGE RATES, AND DOMESTIC PRICE LEVELS

The use of gold, silver, and other precious metals as the basis for money stretches far back in history. The essential characteristic of a gold (or precious metal) standard is the definition of a monetary unit as a fixed weight of gold and the free conversion of currency into gold at the fixed price. In the United States the dollar was initially defined in terms of both gold and silver (a bimetallic standard), though generally only one type of coin circulated. An ounce of gold was worth $19.29 until 1834 when Congress devalued the dollar to $20.67 per ounce of gold, where it remained for the next century. By the late nineteenth century the United States was effectively on a gold standard. Anyone who mined gold could have the gold minted into gold coins at one of the two United States' mints for a very small fee. One ounce, half-ounce, and quarter-ounce gold coins circulated in the United States.

Gold, however, is heavy and not particularly convenient as a means of payment. By the 1870s much of the gold in the United States was deposited in banks in exchange for demand deposits. National banks had to have their capital (initial operating funds) deposited in gold, and most of this was then deposited with the comptroller of the currency who issued government bonds to the national banks. These bonds carried the right to issue currency—national banknotes. The bonds were redeposited with the comptroller of the currency, and national banknotes of nearly the same value as the bonds were printed and given to the bank. A national bank could then issue these national banknotes as currency to depositors and when making loans. Until 1933 depositors had the right to demand that a bank liquidate their accounts and give them in gold the value of the dollars in the accounts. But between 1864 and 1914 most people considered the national banknotes, or currency, as good as gold, and were quite satisfied to receive currency when they withdrew funds from their bank accounts. People who held a bank's currency, or the national banknotes of that bank, could also demand that the bank convert the currency they held into gold.

The United States was not the only country on a gold standard. At the start of the twentieth century most other nations had adopted it. Under the leadership of Great Britain, the period from 1880 through 1914 is considered the heyday of the gold standard. The British defined one ounce of gold as 4.25 pounds sterling while the United States defined one ounce of gold as \$20.67, and both nations stood ready to redeem their currencies in gold at these fixed rates. The result was a fixed rate at which dollars could be exchanged for pounds and vice versa—a rate of \$4.86 per pound or approximately 0.2058 pounds per dollar. Because most countries defined their money in gold at a fixed rate and stood ready to redeem their currencies for gold at the fixed rate, the exchange rates between nearly all the world's currencies were fixed. And this world of fixed exchange rates, operating through the gold standard, was the framework within which the world's international trade took place.

To see how this worked, consider the following example. Suppose that in the early 1890s British importers purchased \$10 million in wheat from American grain exporters. The British would pay for the wheat with exactly 2,057,613.17 pounds sterling. Of course, the American grain exporters could not use British pounds to pay their workers and other bills, nor to buy wheat from American farmers—for this they needed dollars. They would go into the foreign exchange market, sell the 2,057,613.17 British pounds, and receive \$10 million because of the fixed exchange rate of \$4.86 per pound. The buyers of the British pounds might have been several different firms. One firm might have wished to import some steel rails from Britain for the Pennsylvania Railroad. Another might have wanted to purchase British consols (government bonds) as a financial investment. Another might have wished to use British pounds to purchase several tons of coffee from exporters in British Honduras. Ultimately all the British pounds would be recycled and sent back to Great Britain in exchange for commodities (such as cotton and woolen cloth, steel, machinery and equipment, etc.) and investments, such as an investment in the Wilkinson Steel Company or the purchase of bonds issued by the British government or a British corporation.

Suppose, however, that at the British prices prevailing at the time there were insufficient demands from American importers of commodities to use all of the British pounds received by American exporters, and that Americans did not wish to hold British currency or buy British real or financial assets. In other words, there was a commodity trade deficit in British foreign trade and, correspondingly, a commodity trade surplus in American foreign trade. Because the British always stood ready to redeem their pounds for gold, and because the prices of British commodities and assets were "too high" for American purchasers, Americans would begin redeeming British pounds for gold and importing the gold into the United States. Great Britain would now begin to lose gold. As long as the British followed the rules of the gold standard, a loss of gold required them to reduce their money supply. As the money supply in Britain shrank, the prices of British goods and services would fall. This deflation would reduce price levels in Britain. In the United States, meanwhile, the exact opposite would be happening. Gold imported from Britain would increase the money supply, and rising spending would begin to cause rising prices.

The rise in prices of American commodities relative to

commodities in other countries, especially Great Britain, would make them less desirable to foreign buyers, and exports from the United States would begin to fall. The fall in the prices of British commodities would make them more attractive to foreign buyers, and exports from Britain would begin to rise. This would reduce the British trade deficit that had led to the export of gold from Britain, at the same time reducing the American trade surplus that had led Americans to import gold from Britain. The process would continue until American prices had risen sufficiently and British prices had fallen sufficiently to eliminate the trade deficit. Under a gold standard, if the countries follow its rules, domestic price levels will adjust so as to balance trade between countries.

The gold standard before World War I worked relatively well but not quite as smoothly as suggested above. By the late nineteenth century central banks, such as the Bank of England, regularly intervened to counteract some of the monetary effects of the workings of the gold standard. No country held gold reserves sufficient to back up its entire currency supply; a typical ratio was about 40 percent, and most nations' central banks tried to keep some gold reserves in excess of that figure to allow for losses without the need for domestic price and output adjustments. If a disturbance caused a country temporarily to lose gold, its central bank could intervene to raise interest rates, making securities more attractive than gold.

As long as the disturbance was temporary, it created no problems. If more permanent adjustments were required, the continued higher interest rates would begin to reduce domestic investment, causing economic activity to decline, unemployment to rise, and prices to fall. Consequent adjustments would then allow the central bank to reduce its interest rates. Not all prices fell at the same rate nor at the same time, but the system would work essentially according to the basic model.

In addition, central banks did not always allow increases in the gold supply to result in increases in the money supply, and, ultimately, increases in the price level. Increasingly they intervened to "sterilize" the new gold and increase excess gold reserves. Such asymmetrical adjustments were a feature of the 1920s but they were also common in the pre–World War I era. The growing flow of international investment also meant that commodity trade deficits and surpluses might persist for long periods of time. For example, the United States posted international trade deficits—buying more foreign commodities and services than it sold overseas—for most of the late nineteenth century, but it enjoyed offsetting surpluses in capital exports since other countries (Britain in particular) bought real and financial U.S. assets. The gold standard worked relatively well because trade surpluses and deficits were relatively small and required no large adjustments in the price levels between countries. Central banks were generally able to coordinate their actions and control the money supply through the domestic banking systems.

WORLD WAR I DISLOCATIONS AND THE 1920–1921 DEPRESSION

The start of the world war in 1914 brought a quick suspension of the gold standard in the countries involved in the war. Although nominally maintaining their commitments to the gold standard and the system of fixed exchange rates, they effectively left the gold standard through controls, confiscation of circulating gold coins, and other devices. Unconstrained by the gold standard, belligerent countries printed new currency that produced price inflation. Initially these countries turned to the United States to buy war materials. American securities held by citizens and firms in the warring countries were taken over by the governments, brought to the

United States, and sold for dollars to buy munitions, weapons, and other supplies. England, France, Belgium, and other countries also shipped gold to the United States to exchange for dollars to buy war materials. Finally, with the assistance of the U.S. government, Allied countries began selling bonds to American private investors to obtain dollars. With the entrance of the United States into the war in 1917, the U.S. government made loans direct to Allied nations.

Throughout the nineteenth century the United States had been a net debtor with respect to the rest of the world. By 1916 it had been transformed to a net creditor and remained that way until the early 1980s. In 1913 the United States held gold reserves of $1.29 billion, about 26 percent of the world's monetary gold stock. By 1918 American monetary gold stocks had more than doubled to $2.66 billion, about 40 percent of the world's monetary gold.

The dislocations caused by the war were extraordinary. Budgets of European nations were disrupted, and old ideas about spending and taxes were torn apart. Industrial production and patterns of international trade were irrevocably altered. Agricultural production, particularly of grains, in the United States, Canada, Argentina, and Australia grew sharply to compensate for the loss of European production. Non-European industrial production expanded as the United States exported to many countries that had relied on French and British exports, and Japan became a major exporter of industrial products to other Asian countries.

Inflation affected all countries as gold coins were withdrawn from circulation to become part of the gold reserves backing up currency and deposits, except in the United States. The increase in monetary gold stocks led to increases in the money supply even in noncombatant countries. In the United States the price level in 1919 was about twice what it had been in 1913. As they went off the gold standard, the European combatants simply began printing currency that was not backed up by gold. Bereft of an anchor in gold, these countries saw even greater price inflation. Between 1913 and 1919, prices in Britain rose two and a half times, in France three times, and in Germany eight times. No country, in Europe or elsewhere, was immune to the price inflation of the World War I era, but the rate of inflation varied sharply.

Virtually all countries agreed that the gold standard and the fixed exchange rate had to be restored after World War I. There was less agreement on whether the prewar exchange rates should be restored or whether countries should recognize the depreciation of their currencies against gold that had occurred between 1914 and 1918. The United States had maintained its exchange rate even though its price levels had doubled because its gold reserves had doubled. But Britain too wished to return to gold at its prewar parity of $4.86 per pound sterling. To do so required that it obtain additional gold or suffer a sharp price deflation. Countries realized that these issues had to be settled before there was any hope of restoring the gold standard. As a temporary measure, the countries settled on freely floating exchange rates. The pound quickly fell to $3.81 while the German mark and French franc declined even more dramatically against the dollar. During this period of floating exchange rates many countries experienced, in varying degrees, a boom from 1919 into 1920 and a contraction from 1920 to 1921.

In the United States the contraction was short but severe, and was followed by a quick recovery. To assist the Treasury in floating the rest of its war bonds in 1919, the Federal Reserve System, which had excess (or free) gold reserves, had kept its discount rate low for member banks. As banks increased their borrowing, the money supply rose faster and price inflation accelerated. With the final floating of the war bonds in the late fall of 1919, the Federal Reserve System began raising the discount rate. Between November and late January 1920 the rate was raised from 4 to 6 and then to 7 percent on June 1, 1920. The expansion of the money supply during the inflation of 1919 had wiped out much of the Federal Reserve System's free (or excess) gold, and it was determined to restore it by reducing "excess" money. The dramatic increase in the discount rate quickly led banks to cease borrowing and begin paying back loans from the Federal Reserve System. The money supply contracted, market interest rates rose, prices fell very sharply, and the economy suffered a severe depression between mid-1920 and mid-1921. The Federal Reserve System began to reduce the discount rate in June 1921, and by December that year it had fallen to 4.5 percent.

Prices and wage rates had fallen quickly in the 1920–1921 contraction, but the economy quickly recovered and by 1923 was again at full employment. In the Great Depression, Federal Reserve officials expected the same type of price and wage flexibility as in 1920–1921. Officials in countries around the world looked at the instability associated with the inflation and deflation (the "boom and slump") of 1919–1921 that had occurred under floating exchange rates and became convinced of the necessity of returning to a gold standard and to fixed exchange rates. They did not see that the floating exchange rates gave them a cushion from the effects of policies and events in other countries. Floating exchange rates provided some isolation from the policies of the U.S. Federal Reserve System. Germany, Austria, and Poland did not follow the United States in the 1920–1921 depression, and Britain also largely avoided it. The episode was less severe for other countries that only partially emulated the policies of the United States. Under a fixed-rate, gold standard regime, that partial isolation would be lost—as they would discover during the Great Depression.

WAR DEBTS, WAR REPARATIONS, AND RESTORING THE GOLD STANDARD

European conferences on restoring the gold standard met at Brussels in 1920 and at Genoa two years later. One critical issue they debated was whether currencies should be stabilized at new, lower exchange rates to reflect wartime inflation or at prewar rates. If stabilization was to be at prewar levels, countries would have to endure long, slow deflations and almost certainly higher levels of unemployment and slower real growth. If they stabilized at the lower postwar parities, there would be no deflation, unemployment, or slower growth. But investors might not view this approach as a credible commitment to the gold standard and would certainly be reminded that governments reserved the right to change the domestic price of gold as they saw fit.

By the beginning of the 1920s the United States held 40 percent of the world's monetary gold reserves. With that distribution of gold and without a worldwide deflation, there was far too little gold to support restoration at prewar rates—not even enough to support restoration at postwar rates. A proposal was made to create a gold exchange standard whereby key gold-standard countries would hold gold reserves sufficient to support their liabilities while other countries would hold international reserves composed of a combination of gold and of currencies of the key gold-standard countries, the United States and Great Britain. Approved in 1922, this was how the restored gold standard of the 1920s developed—as a gold exchange standard.

Other problems also confronted the conferences. The victorious Allies, principally Britain, Belgium, and France, demanded that Germany make reparations payments in gold marks to defray their cost of the war. Germany had planned to make similar demands if it won the war. The amounts demanded and finally settled on were enormous, causing considerable doubt in many quarters that the German economy would be able to make such payments. The United States refused to be a party to the demands for reparations payments. But Washington did ask that European nations pay their war debts incurred before the United States entered the war. The European nations contended that they needed reparations payments from Germany to do this, even though the United States opposed reparations payments.

German Hyperinflation of 1922–1923

Between 1919 and 1921 contentious debate over German reparations festered. In London in 1921 it was agreed that the reparations bill was an enormous 132 billion gold marks (or $31 billion), and that annual payments of 4 billion gold marks toward 50 billion gold marks of reparations, occupations costs, and prewar debt were to begin that year. Payment on the remaining 82 billion gold marks was postponed until Germany had the capacity to pay.

The only way that Germany could accumulate that amount of gold was to run an export surplus and receive the surplus in gold from nations buying German exports. The scheduled reparations payments represented about 80 percent of Germany's exports in 1921–1922, but expanding German exports required more imports for German industry. Moreover, Germany's export strengths lay in iron, steel, textiles, and coal, industries that France, Great Britain, Belgium, the United States, and other developed countries considered keys to their economies. They had protected these products from import competition in the past, and they did so again in the early 1920s by raising protective tariff barriers. But by linking reparations payments to the strength of the German economy, negotiators reduced German officials' incentives to take the difficult steps necessary to raise the massive reparations payments. At the same time the victorious continental Allies were adamant that they needed reparations in order to make debt payments to the United States, which refused to forgive their war debts. All of this set the stage for one of the worst hyperinflations in history.

A hyperinflation is a geometrically accelerating rate of price inflation. In the German hyperinflation of 1922–1923 the inflation rate was very closely tied to the depreciation of the mark against the American dollar, the world's strongest currency. Here was the exchange rate between the German mark and the American dollar at selected dates:

January 1913:	4.2 marks per dollar
January 1919:	8.9
January 1922:	191.8
June 1922:	350
October 1922:	4,500
January 1923:	18,000
November 1923:	4.2 trillion

Increasing government deficits led the German government to order the Reichsbank to print more money to finance the shortfalls, and this fed the hyperinflation. Germany became more reluctant to solve the inflation problem after troops from France and Belgium occupied the Ruhr in January 1923. People refused to hold the rapidly depreciating mark. Prices began to be quoted in U.S. dollars, and buyers and sellers had to check the exchange rate to determine the mark value of what they were buying. People holding cash and financial assets were hit especially hard by the hyperinflation, while those holding assets whose values could easily change—for example, land and steel mills—lost less. Some even gained. The impact on the middle class entailed severe political consequences, because Germany never fully recovered from its 1920s hyper-inflation. Economic activity began to contract as the hyperinflation continued. In November 1923 the government gained greater control of its budget, reduced the deficit, and stopped monetizing the deficit through the Reichsbank. Ultimately the reichsmark replaced the mark; it took 4.2 billion marks to buy 1 reichsmark.

Because of their ties to the German economy, the Austrian, Hungarian, and Polish economies also experienced inflation in 1922–1923, though it was less severe than Germany's. The German hyperinflation had a lasting impact. Officials in European countries reiterated their vows to return to the gold standard to control inflation, which was never far from their thoughts. In 1936 even the U.S. Federal Reserve System took contractionary measures to reduce the potential for inflation despite an unemployment level of 13 to 14 percent.

At the end of 1923 Germany was in no condition to make reparations payments, and by 1924 it was generally conceded that the scheduled reparations payments were unrealistic. A committee was formed under the leadership of Charles Dawes of the United States to evaluate the reparations problem. The Dawes Plan drastically scaled back the reparations to about 1 percent of German national income in 1924, with scheduled increases to 1929 as long as the German economy could support them. To aid the stabilization of the German government, a loan of 800 million gold marks was arranged, with the bulk of the bonds marketed in New York. The success of this loan unleashed a wave of American lending to Germany, Central European countries, and Central and South American countries from 1925 through 1928. These loans became crucial to the functioning of the international economy. Dollars from American loans to Germany provided the basis for the growth of the German economy and German reparations payments to Britain, Belgium, France, and Italy. These countries then used those dollars to make payments on their war debts to the United States. Thus the dollars sent overseas as loans made their way back to the United States. The system worked as long as nothing interrupted this flow.

THE GOLD STANDARD RESTORED, 1925–1929

Lacking a consensus on how to return to a gold standard, countries used different strategies. European countries that had experienced less inflation over the war years chose to undergo deflation (reduced price levels) in order to return to gold at prewar parities. In Great Britain, the Bank of England raised interest rates to reduce price levels and obtain additional monetary gold from abroad. This resulted in higher unemployment, less investment, and slower growth, but Britain returned to gold in 1925 at the prewar parity of $4.86 per pound sterling. Sweden, the Netherlands, Denmark, and Norway returned to the prewar parities by undergoing deflation.

Other European countries had experienced greater rates of price inflation in the war years and the 1920s. France, for example, had barely escaped hyperinflation when it reached an inflation rate of 350 percent per year in June 1926. Belgium, anticipating German reparations payments, allowed its budget to go into deficit and then monetized the resulting debt by printing paper money. Czechoslovakia, Italy, and Portugal had also experienced greater rates of inflation; they were also unwilling to undergo the necessary deflation and chose to return to gold at less than prewar parities. France, the other major economy and gold-standard country, stabilized its currency in late 1926 and formally returned to the gold standard in June 1928. The French franc exchanged at 124 to the pound sterling and 25.51 to the dollar when stabilized. Before the war the exchange rates had been 25 francs to the pound and 5 francs to the dollar. By 1929, forty-five nations around the globe had adopted the gold exchange standard. The United States and Great Britain were the major currencies standing ready to exchange their currencies for gold. Other countries supplemented their monetary gold reserves with pounds and dollars.

The gold exchange standard suffered from serious problems. Everywhere prices and money supplies were much higher than they had been before the war, but the world's gold stocks had not grown much. To centralize gold in monetary gold stocks, most countries had stopped allowing gold coins to circulate. But there simply was not enough monetary gold to support money supplies at prewar parities. And during the 1920s the United States accumulated 40 or more percent of the world's gold compared to 25 to 26 percent before the war. To return to gold at prewar parities would have required countries everywhere to undergo significant deflation. They were also unwilling to return to gold at the depreciated parities of the 1920s. The compromise, the gold exchange standard, attempted to allow a return to gold despite the fact that there was far too little of the precious metal to support the world's currencies at prewar parities. If several countries attempted to convert their dollar and pound sterling reserves into gold, as the gold standard allowed, the system would quickly collapse because of inadequate monetary gold reserves.

Britain's return to gold at the prewar parity left the pound overvalued relative to other currencies. The prices of British exports were thus too high relative to foreign prices, leading to fewer exports. The prices of British imports were lower relative to the prices of British goods, leading to more imports into Britain. To support the overvalued pound, the Bank of England kept interest rates high to halt an outflow of gold reserves. When France returned to gold the franc was undervalued (the reverse of the British pound) and, like a magnet, this attracted gold. French law largely eliminated open-market operations by the French central bank, and the discount market was relatively small. As a result, gold inflows were largely sterilized (not allowed to increase in the money supply), and the franc continued to be undervalued. By 1927, France had about 9 percent of the world's monetary gold reserves, by 1929 about 17 percent, and by 1931 about 22 percent.

International trade patterns had been disrupted by the war. Many countries formally on the periphery of international trade had expanded their production of foodstuffs and raw materials in response to war demands. After 1924 much of the expanded foreign lending, primarily from the United States, was used to enhance the production of raw materials and foodstuffs. This expanded world production led to declining prices for primary products, putting pressure on trade balances and leading to increased protective measures in various countries.

The two key currencies in the gold exchange standard were the British pound and the American dollar. Britain struggled under the overvalued pound. They were able to return to gold in 1925 only with the assistance of the United States. In 1924 the Federal Reserve System temporarily reduced interest rates while the Bank of England raised its rates. To invest in British assets, international investors sold dollars in the United States for gold, sent the gold to Britain to exchange for pounds, and used the pounds to buy British financial assets. The action sent enough gold into British reserves to allow it to return to the gold standard—and the expansionary monetary policy in the United States worked because the country was experiencing a minor recession. This reduction in interest rates and increase in the money supply due to the Federal Reserve's actions may have been one among many factors sparking the late-twenties boom in the American stock market.

Gold parities around the world were not consistent with the existing distribution of gold, trade patterns, and price levels in various countries. As long as countries were unwilling to adjust exchange rates or to undergo necessary deflation, the gold exchange standard could be maintained only by the continuing coordinated actions of central banks to offset destabilizing gold flows, and by the continued flow of dollars out of the United States through foreign lending. Any disruption would mean trouble for the world economic system.

Destabilizing Gold Flows and Deflationary Policies, 1927–1929

The Great Depression did not begin in the United States. By late 1927 there were signs of economic contraction in Southeast Asia. Germany had problems in the same year. In May 1927 its stock market crashed, and by 1928 it had fallen into depression. So had Brazil. By early 1929 the economies of Poland, Argentina, and Canada were contracting, and by midyear the U.S. economy began shrinking. Inexorably the gold exchange standard began leading to deflation and economic contraction as countries sought to strengthen or maintain their monetary gold reserves.

In early 1927 the Bank of France began to redeem pounds sterling for gold, as the gold exchange standard allowed. France, in the midst of officially returning to the gold standard, needed additional gold reserves and did not wish to hold as much British currency. Because Britain's gold reserves were threatened, France agreed to temporarily stop converting pounds to gold while the Federal Reserve System reduced its discount rate to 3.5 percent—thereby further spurring speculation in the American stock market. The loss of British gold stopped, and some U.S. monetary gold reserves made their way to Britain and, primarily, France. By early 1928 the United States decided that it had lost enough gold. More important, the booming American stock market worried officials of the Federal Reserve System. In early 1928 they took steps to dampen the market and stem the gold outflow by raising the discount rate from 3.5 percent to 4 percent. By July 1928 they had raised the discount rate to 5 percent, and in late 1928 and early 1929 they took additional deflationary steps by selling securities on the open market.

American interest rates quickly shot upward in response to the increase in the discount rate, and gold began to flow into the United States. French gold reserves continued to rise in 1928 as France obtained an additional 3 percent of the world's monetary gold stocks. American foreign lending declined sharply in the last half of 1928, and in 1929 there was little American short-term foreign lending and a sharp decline in American long-term foreign lending. That year high American interest rates and the booming stock market attracted those funds and brought in gold from around the world.

By 1929 most of the nations in the world were losing gold as it flowed into the United States and France. France, however, did not allow its money supply to expand, and during that year the United States continued under the Federal Reserve's deflationary policies. Central banks across the globe raised interest rates and reduced or slowed the growth of money supplies in order to defend gold parities by halting trade deficits and losses of gold. Around the world countries found themselves in the grip of deflationary strategies designed to reduce price levels. In country after country, economic activity contracted as the worldwide Great Depression began.

WHY WAS THE DEPRESSION MORE SEVERE IN THE UNITED STATES?

Compared to previous depressions, the contraction that had begun by 1929 would have been judged as severe because of the strong deflationary policies prevailing in so many countries. But it was not apparent to observers that this would become the Great Depression. Once price levels had been pushed down and unbalanced gold flows had ceased, economies were expected to recover. In the United States, however, the contraction was longer than in most countries and was the most severe on record. Several factors help explain this.

The deflationary impulse in the United States was initially strengthened by the stock market crash. Although the crash was brought on by the downturn in economic activity, it accelerated the decline. The plunge in stock market values generated greater uncertainty about the future and led consumers to reduce their spending on durable goods in late 1929 and early 1930. In addition, consumers had built up large amounts of consumer debt at the end of the 1920s with relatively smaller amounts of financial assets. The stock market crash reduced the value of tangible assets and deteriorated household balance sheets. Consumers were forced to reduce their spending in an effort to rebuild their budgets. As a result, the contraction of economic activity accelerated.

But in this contraction the behavior of wage rates and prices in the first two years was surprisingly different. In the 1920–1921 contraction there had been a rapid and sharp decline in prices and wage rates, resulting in a short, though severe, downturn. Quick deflationary adjustments pushed prices and wage rates down, allowing the economy to begin recovering. But in the first two years of the Great Depression

in the United States, this was not the case. The larger manufacturing firms kept nominal (or current dollar) wage rates
virtually constant through 1930, though there were some reductions in small, competitive firms. Most of the larger manufacturing firms laid off employees and cut workweeks,
allowing their profits to fall, rather than cut wage rates or reduce dividends.

At the time this rigidity of money wage rates in manufacturing was considered highly unusual and was widely
commented on by politicians, business and labor leaders, jour-
nalists, and academics. Many, but not all, considered it a favorable sign. Before the mid-1920s, wages generally fell soon after
economic activity began contracting. Typically in the years
from 1890 to 1924, wage rates fell 9 to 10 percent in a contraction, and contractions averaged a year to eighteen months.
Thus in 1930 observers saw the nearly two-year stability of
manufacturing wages as quite unusual.

Prices, which had fallen slightly in 1928 and 1929, fell faster
in 1930 as the contraction quickened. The All Commodities
Wholesale Price Index in 1930 was 9.6 percent less than in
1929; it declined by 17.1 percent between 1930 and 1931, and a
further 11.25 percent by 1932. The Consumer Price Index,
though not declining as rapidly, fell 2.6 percent between 1929
and 1930, 9.2 percent between 1930 and 1931, and 10.9 percent
between 1931 and 1932. At the same time prices were falling,
real production was also contracting. Real GNP declined 11
percent between 1929 and 1930 and 5.4 percent between 1930
and 1931. Production in the durable manufacturing sector
dropped 36.3 percent between December 1929 and December
1930, and fell an additional 36.2 percent between December
1930 and December 1931.

Thus during 1930 and 1931 prices were falling—especially
wholesale prices, those relevant for manufacturing firms' decisions—and manufacturing output was plunging. Falling
prices and stable wages raised real hourly labor costs for com-

panies by 7.8 percent in 1930 and 9.5 percent in 1931. Their response was to cut production and lay off workers. The unemployment rate rose from an average of 3.2 percent in 1929 to 8.9 percent in 1930 and 16.3 percent in 1931. With rising real wage rates and falling demand, firms had little choice but to begin massive lay offs. The deflation of the first two years of the Great Depression, unlike previous contractions, affected prices but did not change wage rates in a large and important sector.

As 1931 progressed, more large manufacturing firms now began to cut wages. These included Fisher Body, Chrysler, National Cash Register, Firestone, Goodyear, U.S. Rubber, and Westinghouse. The Bureau of Labor Statistics reported 221 wage rate cuts in the last half of July and first half of August 1931. In the fall, over the objections of its president Gerard Swope, the board of directors of General Electric directed the company to initiate wage rate cuts. On October 1, 1931, United States Steel directors disregarded the recommendations of its company president, James A. Farrell, and reduced wage rates by 11 percent. In October 1931, International Harvester cut its common labor wage rates by 15 percent. That same month Henry Ford, who had raised wages at the beginning of 1930, reduced wage rates by 25 percent at Ford Motor Company. By the end of 1931 wage rate cuts of 10 percent or more in manufacturing were common. Cities now began cutting the wage rates and salaries of public employees, sometimes as much as 25 percent. In the spring of 1932 construction workers in New York City and Chicago saw their wage rates cut 25 percent—though, of course, there was little construction activity. Railroads bargained with their unions to cut wage rates by 10 percent. By the fall of 1931 conditions in American manufacturing were so dismal that firms finally resorted to cutting nominal wage rates, and both nominal and real wage rates fell in 1932 and 1933.

Why did firms wait so long to cut nominal wage rates?

Certainly employees resisted wage rate cuts, but they had long objected to them. Bloody strikes were fought over wage rate cuts in the 1890s, but rates were nonetheless cut just as they were in 1907–1908 and 1920–1921. Nor was the delay due to union resistance and union contracts. The percentage of the labor force that was unionized had fallen 50 percent from 1920–1921 (when there were wage rate cuts) to 1929–1930. Neither can implicit contracts between employees and management, or employer worries about higher labor turnover and reduced efficiency, explain this unusual behavior. The explanation lies in the changed attitudes of business leaders and government officials.

Herbert Hoover had been astonished and upset by the wage rate cuts in the 1920–1921 depression. As secretary of commerce he had organized a conference on unemployment to consider how to stop this behavior. Unfortunately for Hoover, the depression ended before the conference could begin, but throughout the 1920s Hoover preached a "high wage" policy and railed against the "liquidation" of labor through wage rate cuts. By the mid-1920s many business leaders, labor leaders, and academics were supporting what was usually called the "high wage" policy. The argument was that if firms paid high wages, their employees would be able to buy the products and services being produced, and firms would thus find "steadier" markets. If firms refused to reduce wage rates during a contraction, their employees would have more income and would spend more, thus helping moderate the contraction. Firms were urged to reduce the length of the workweek rather than lay off their employees. By the mid-1920s such noted industrialists as Walter Teagle of Standard Oil of New Jersey, Owen D. Young of General Electric, Myron Taylor of United States Steel, Alfred P. Sloan, Jr., of General Motors, Julius Rosenwald of Sears, Roebuck, Edward Filene of Filene's Department Stores, Howard Heinz of Heinz Foods, W. R. Wrigley of Wrigley's Gum, and Pierre du Pont of the

Du Pont Company were endorsing the high-wage policy. Academic economists such as Rexford Tugwell, Wesley Claire Mitchell, Leo Wolman, John R. Commons, Paul Douglas, John Bates Clark, and Davis R. Dewey supported the new concept.

The Hawley-Smoot tariff also aided the high-wage policy. Tariffs protect firms from foreign competition, allowing them to pay higher wages and maintain higher prices for their products. It was 1932 before the effects of the tariff were really felt in the American economy, and even then it was of secondary importance in supporting the high-wage policy. But although the tariff was not passed until early 1930, by November 1929 it was clear that it would be enacted, and Hoover and the industrialists understood what the role of the tariff was.

Thus in December 1929, when President Hoover urged industrialists to maintain wage rates and spread the work among employees, it is hardly surprising that they responded by publicly agreeing to hold the line on wages. To renege on such a public commitment in the spring or summer or even the fall of 1930 would have been a public embarrassment. Some work was spread, but the economic decline was so severe that increasing layoffs were necessary. By 1931 even these larger manufacturing firms realized that wage cuts were essential. The maintenance of money wage rates distorted relative prices and thwarted the deflation objectives of the Federal Reserve System. If wage rates had been cut as prices fell, the contraction would likely have been much shorter than it turned out to be. The initial downturn was not as rapid in 1929–1930 as it was in 1920–1921; the difference was in the rigidity of money wage rates.

FEDERAL RESERVE POLICY

In contrast to wages, there was no systematic pressure to maintain prices of commodities and services at the wholesale and retail levels. In fact, officials at the Federal Reserve System believed it desirable for prices to fall in accord with the rules of the gold standard. Therefore prices fell during the first two years of the contraction because the Federal Reserve System allowed the money supply to decline. The Federal Reserve had held the discount rate at 6 percent in September and October 1929. With the stock market crash, the discount rate was reduced to 4.5 percent and then, in a series of steps, to 1.5 percent by April 1931. Although the New York Federal Reserve Bank had purchased securities to provide cash to New York City banks during and directly after the crash, this was quickly withdrawn and no further open-market operations were conducted. Banks began to repay their borrowings from the Federal Reserve Banks. Although there was some gold inflow, it was not enough to offset the reduction in bank borrowing at the discount window, and from August 1929 through August 1931 bank reserves and the money supply declined. Because market interest rates had fallen to relatively low levels and banks' excess reserves grew, officials at the Federal Reserve System believed that monetary policy was already "easy." They were generally following the guidelines of the gold standard, and under this framework there was nothing wrong with a little deflation.

Ordinarily such a decline in the discount rate should have led member banks to borrow from the Federal Reserve in order to make additional loans to their customers. But these were not ordinary times. Short-term interest rates, such as on commercial paper, fell by about the same amount and at the same time as the discount rate. Banks did not find it worthwhile to borrow from the Federal Reserve in order to relend in the short-term market. Between the close of 1929 and the summer of 1931, as the economy collapsed, investment demands from bank borrowers shrank and bank loans to businesses became increasingly risky. This made banks more and more reluctant to lend to businesses. Thus the decreases in the

Federal Reserve's discount rate did not have the anticipated effect in stimulating borrowing and business activity between the end of 1929 and the summer of 1931.

Bank failures began to rise in 1930 and increased in November with the failure of Caldwell and Company. Many of these were also related to the high-wage policy. As firms held wage rates constant during 1930, they also tried to maintain their dividend payments as Hoover had advocated in December 1929. The administration's approach was to let the first shock of the contraction fall on business profits. Dividend payments in 1930 were nearly 95 percent as large as they had been in 1929. But undistributed corporate profits fell sharply, from about $2.8 billion in 1929 to a negative $2.6 billion in 1930. The value of these firms' securities held by banks also began falling. The deterioration in banks' portfolios and the decline in banks' capital led to steadily worsening financial conditions of the banks. Investors were the first to see this, and in 1930 share prices of banks fell sharply. In fact, evidence suggests that the value of bank stocks fell faster than the value of major industrial stocks.

By the end of 1930 banks and their depositors began to respond to the evidence of the increasing risks of bank failure. Banks began systematically to increase their reserves relative to deposits. Depositors began to hold more and more currency relative to deposits. Both these trends continued through March 1933. Fractional reserve banking now began to work its magic. The loss of banks' reserves, as depositors increasingly held more currency and less deposits, required a contraction of the money supply. The increasing reserve ratios of banks reinforced this trend. This shrinkage was partially offset by an increase in reserves due to the flow of gold into the United States through September 1931. But the net effect was a pronounced and relentless contraction of the money supply.

INTERNATIONAL DEVELOPMENTS

In October 1931 the gold exchange standard again brought its vengeance down upon the United States. As the banking disturbance in Austria spread to Central Europe and Germany, these countries effectively left the gold standard. Lenders to these countries, who saw their assets frozen, wanted safer, more liquid assets—gold. According to the gold exchange standard, the key countries, Great Britain and the United States, stood ready to redeem their currencies—held as international reserves by other countries—for gold. And central bankers turned to Great Britain to do just that. But under the gold exchange standard there simply were not enough gold reserves, given the countries' money supplies and price levels. Britain could redeem its currency for gold and remain on the gold standard only by undergoing a severe deflation of prices and wages. Unwilling to do this, in September 1931 Britain abandoned the gold standard.

Other countries now turned to the United States to honor its commitment to gold, and the Federal Reserve System had to respond. The flow of gold out of the United States in September and especially October amounted to $725 million—which roughly offset all of the net inflows of gold in the previous two years. As gold left the United States, the Federal reserve could begin to reduce bank reserves consistent with the loss of gold, or it could reduce the gold outflow by raising interest rates. It chose to raise the discount rate from 1.5 percent to 3.5 percent. Market interest rates shot upward and the gold outflow stopped; a small flow of gold back to the United States even occurred. The Federal Reserve System had no authority to leave the gold standard; only the president and Congress could make that decision. The Federal Reserve could temporarily suspend the gold reserve requirement but chose not to do so. Presumably this was because not all the regional Federal Reserve Banks had lost gold, and some might object to this action because it was not a longer-term solution to the loss of gold. The result was a more rapid decline in prices, production, and employment in late 1931 and early 1932. Bond prices fell as interest rates rose, causing the financial condition of banks (who were holding more bonds as the demand for loans shrank) to deteriorate more rapidly. The result was a sharp surge in bank failures in late 1931 and early 1932, with frozen deposits that produced further economic contraction. In the first six months of 1931, the unemployment rate had been 14 to 15 percent. By December 1931 it was nearly 20 percent, and by June 1932 it was nearly 26 percent. Between December 1931 and June 1932 durable manufacturing production declined 30 percent. Between 1931 and 1932 wholesale prices declined more than 11 percent while consumer prices declined nearly 11 percent. Any positive effects that could have arisen due to the initiation of wage cuts were swept away by the Federal Reserve's powerful contractionary monetary policy to preserve the gold standard.

FEDERAL RESERVE OPEN-MARKET PURCHASES

By January 1932 the Federal Reserve Banks, especially the New York Bank, had few reserves of free gold. Member banks' discounting of eligible securities had declined, and the banks had to use what would have been free gold reserves (in excess of the required 40 percent backing member banks' reserve deposits and outstanding Federal Reserve currency) to meet the requirement of 60 percent of Federal Reserve currency backed by eligible securities or gold. As part of a plan to halt price deflation and ease credit conditions, the government created the Reconstruction Finance Corporation to lend to banks to stabilize their capital structure, and in late February

1932 passed the Glass-Steagall Act authorizing the Federal Reserve System to use federal government securities as additional backing for outstanding Federal Reserve notes. As federal government securities—primarily short-term securities—were purchased, gold backing up currency would be released to augment free gold and, if necessary, be exported to meet foreign demands.

Only small amounts of securities were purchased in March, but in April 1932 the Federal Reserve System began to use this new authority. Over the next fourteen weeks it engaged in open-market purchases that doubled its holdings of short-term government securities. These purchases were three times the magnitude of any previous open-market purchases and increased bank reserves and publicly held currency by 12 percent. The purchases ended suddenly in July 1932. Federal Reserve Bank officials observed increasing reserves in member banks and no rise in member bank borrowing (this had largely ceased at the beginning of 1932). According to Federal Reserve standards, monetary policy was already very easy; further purchases would be of little use because member banks would simply increase their excess reserves rather than expand credit. Chicago Federal Reserve Bank directors were among those who pointed this out and in July the Chicago, Boston, and Philadelphia banks all pulled out of the open-market purchases program. The directors of the New York Federal Reserve Bank did not believe that they could carry on with the purchases largely on their own. Chicago and Boston officials were also worried that their member banks were threatened because they held larger amounts of short-term government securities, and the open-market purchases pushed up the securities' prices, reducing the earnings on them. This reduced the earnings of those member banks.

Although reserves of member banks and currency held by the general public continued to grow in the last five months of

1932 as gold flowed into the United States, the rate of growth was about half what it was while the program of open-market purchases was in place. The open-market purchases did appear to have a favorable effect. Stock market prices bottomed out in the summer of 1932 and then began rising. The money supply stopped falling and increased 2 percent between August and November 1932. Between July and November industrial production increased 12 percent, and in the last quarter of 1932 the unemployment rate declined. These were signs of recovery that gave Hoover some hope going into the fall presidential election. They might have been stronger if the open-market purchases had continued. Even the April-to-July change in policy might have been sufficient if the last burst of the monetary tornado had not swept through the United States between December 1932 and the beginning of March 1933.

THE FINAL BANKING PANIC

By December 1932 the uncertainty surrounding the plans of newly elected President Franklin Delano Roosevelt had stalled the recovery. Industrial production had stopped growing in November and fell slightly in December. The unemployment rate, which tended to lag behind other changes, continued to fall into December but rose after that. In January 1933 the public began systematically to convert deposits into currency as information about banks receiving Reconstruction Finance Loans was released. As more banks failed, new problems arose.

Roosevelt had refused to deny or confirm rumors that he would devalue the dollar. As farmers and farm organizations continued their calls for devaluation to aid the ailing farm economy, Roosevelt met with Professor George Warren, an outspoken advocate of devaluation. In mid-February, Congress directed the Treasury to issue silver certificates by buying silver at above-market prices. Carter Glass turned down the position of Treasury secretary because Roosevelt refused to pledge that he would not devalue the dollar. The result was an increase in the demand for gold, some of which was certainly domestic but most of which was foreign. Foreign conversion of currency into gold accelerated, and Eastern Federal Reserve Banks, chiefly the New York Bank, bore the brunt of this conversion. Between February 1 and March 4 the New York Bank lost 61 percent of its gold reserves; on March 3 its gold reserves were less than half of the foreign deposits in New York City banks. By the beginning of March the conversion of currency into gold began to significantly reduce the gold reserve of the Boston, Philadelphia, and Chicago Federal Reserve Banks. Though other banks had free gold, they were unwilling to provide gold to the New York Bank by discounting (buying for gold) the government securities held by the New York Bank. By Friday, March 3, New York Federal Reserve Bank Governor George Harrison was convinced that not only would the bank's gold reserves fall well below the required minimum, but conversions would wipe out all its reserves. The Chicago Federal Reserve Bank had also come under great stress at the end of February as its gold reserves declined by 15 percent between February 21 and March 1. On Saturday, March 4, the governors of New York and Illinois declared bank holidays in their states, effectively shutting down the American financial system. In four months this last financial panic had reduced the money supply by 7.3 percent, the unemployment rate had risen from 22.3 to 28.3 percent, and manufacturing production had plunged 18 percent. Roosevelt's nationwide bank holiday extended the shutdown to the eighteen states that had not yet done so.

3

The First New Deal, 1933–1935

"LET ME ASSERT my firm belief that the only thing we have to fear is, fear itself—nameless, unreasoning, unjustified terror which paralyzes needed efforts to convert retreat into advance." These famous words were part of the opening remarks in Franklin Delano Roosevelt's call to wage war on the Great Depression. The struggle to bring recovery to the American economy and simultaneously to reform it would consume Roosevelt and his advisers for the remainder of the 1930s. Because FDR played such a pivotal and personal role in these events, it is important to know who this man was.

Roosevelt was the only son of James and Sara Delano Roosevelt. He was born into wealth and received much of his education from private tutors at the Roosevelts' Hyde Park estate on the Hudson River, eighty miles north of New York City. Sheltered from much of the world by an overly protective mother, Franklin was sent to Groton, an elite preparatory school, to finish his education before enrolling at Harvard University. Although he was popular and active in student government and athletics, he was a rather indifferent student. After Harvard he studied law at Columbia University but dropped out before receiving a degree. He managed to pass the bar exams but soon found he was not interested in private practice. With his patrician upbringing, politics seemed his gentlemanly calling, and in 1910 he was elected to the New York Senate. As a rising star in progressive Democratic politics and an active supporter of Woodrow Wilson, Roosevelt received his due reward when Wilson named him assistant secretary of the navy in 1913. He remained at this post for the next seven years. In 1920 the Democratic party nominated him for vice president on the ticket headed by James Cox, but they lost badly in the election.

His budding political career was set back when in 1921 he contracted poliomyelitis. He underwent a long rehabilitation but for the rest of his life was paralyzed from the waist down. By the late 1920s he was ready to resume his political career, and in 1928 he was elected governor of New York and re-elected in 1930. Roosevelt was a polished speaker and a consummate politician, and he attracted much attention in his gubernatorial position, using it as the springboard to the Democratic party's presidential nomination in 1932.

Roosevelt's sheltered upbringing in the world of the wealthy influenced his view and his approach to the world. Gentlemen aimed to win, but to win within the rules of whatever game they were engaged in—to win as good sportsmen win. One should be concerned for the welfare of others and not overly concerned with attempting to increase one's wealth if it might harm others. This view would influence FDR's 1936 attack on the "royalists," the powerful business interests who sought to thwart his programs to improve society. He never fully understood why businessmen were so reluctant to give up a little of their power and wealth to the less privileged.

Roosevelt was not a deep thinker—he was a politician. He surveyed every action from a political point of view. His advisers developed his programs, and he left it to them to work out the details. He sold his programs through his ability to charm and persuade people. In the midst of the greatest economic crisis in world history, Roosevelt understood little about how the economic world functioned and little about economic ideas. He appreciated common sense and often ridiculed the expert or the theoretician. But he was a skilled negotiator and extraordinarily adept at manipulating power. Few could mold and use public opinion as well as FDR, and from the beginning he had the support and confidence of the American people.

THE NEW DEAL

Roosevelt was one of the first presidents to draw his advisers heavily from the academic world. Some of them accompanied him from New York to Washington. His closest adviser and confidant at the start of his administration was Louis M. Howe, a former journalist who was perhaps the most influential person close to the president and also provided some restraint on Roosevelt's penchant for quick judgment. As governor of New York, Roosevelt had appointed social worker Frances Perkins as the first woman to head the state's Industrial Commission. When he went to Washington, he appointed Perkins secretary of labor. She helped develop and implement important labor legislation, including the Wagner Act, the Fair Labor Standards Act, and the Social Security Act. Harry Hopkins was another social worker who in 1931 helped administer relief in New York City. Impressed with Hopkins's work, Roosevelt brought him to Washington where he administered a massive federal relief effort in the winter of 1933–1934.

Another group of advisers were sometimes called the "brains trust." They were chiefly Columbia University professors who had begun to counsel Roosevelt while he was governor of New York. Raymond Moley taught public law in Columbia's political science department. He advocated cooperation between government and business, a goal that required government intervention and the reform of business practices to promote socially responsible planning.

Adolf A. Berle was a law professor at Columbia. In his 1932 book with Gardiner Means, *The Modern Corporation and Private Property*, he argued that the growth of large corporations had effectively separated the ownership of these corporations (the stockholders) from their control, allowing the managers to pursue goals other than maximum profits (such as maximizing growth or market share or the incomes of operating officers). Berle proposed that corporate managers take a broader view of their social responsibilities. When he became a New Dealer, he argued for greater federal government influence over large corporations through planning that incorporated broader social responsibilities.

Rexford Tugwell, an economics professor at Columbia, specialized in agricultural economics and was considered a somewhat more radical planner than Moley and Berle. Tugwell believed that uncontrolled markets were a chaotic means of organizing an economy and usually concentrated the benefits of market activity on those who controlled the firms in those markets. Tugwell's solution was a collectivist type of national economic planning. M. L. Wilson of Montana State College was another specialist in farm economics who joined the discussion of agricultural problems. Harold Ickes, a liberal Republican lawyer from Chicago, was brought in to head the Department of the Interior and to direct the new Public Works Administration.

ENDING THE FINANCIAL CRISIS

As Roosevelt took office the nation's financial system seemed to be imploding. Despite President Hoover's pleas, on the morning of Saturday, March 4, 1933, the governors of New York and Illinois both declared bank holidays. Chicago, with the largest commodity exchange, and New York City, with the largest securities markets, were America's financial centers. Many rural and city banks had correspondent deposits in Chicago and New York City banks to handle transactions and earn interest income on what might otherwise have been idle cash balances. These deposits that still remained there were now frozen. As the banking system closed down, payment by check became impossible. Individuals and businesses could not convert deposits into cash. Restarting the nation's financial system was clearly the most immediate and crucial task facing Roosevelt's new administration.

Roosevelt's first action, on Sunday, March 5, 1933, was to order all the nation's banks and thrift institutions closed until Thursday, March 9. He invoked the Trading with the Enemy Act to justify this action and called for a special session of Congress to meet on Thursday. At that session Congress passed the Emergency Banking Act, confirming the new president's initiatives and giving him full authority to solve the nation's financial crisis.

The reopening of the nation's banks was postponed until the banks were examined. Banks that were found to be unsound could be reorganized or merged into a sound bank. To aid this scheme, the Reconstruction Finance Corporation could subscribe to new issues of a bank's preferred stock so that it could be reorganized or reopened. To provide additional money, the Federal Reserve System was authorized to issue currency with only government securities as backing for the notes. To help banks that needed cash, the Federal Reserve System was also authorized to lend on a wider range of assets than had previously been acceptable. Confirming some people's fears, Roosevelt also moved to alter the gold standard, the basis for the money supply in the United States and for foreign exchange. The government now was empowered to control all foreign exchange transactions and all gold and currency movements into and out of the United States. Banks that were allowed to reopen were prohibited from paying out gold or gold certificates.

With this emergency bill and auditors' examinations, the banks began to reopen. Sound banks in the 12 Federal Reserve cities reopened on Monday, March 13, one week after the initial closing. The next day sound banks in 250 cities with clearinghouses for the banks of the city were allowed to reopen. On Wednesday, March 15, sound banks in other cities were reopened. Banks in smaller cities and towns were reopened as they were found to be sound or were reorganized or merged into sound banks. Eleven days after the initial closing of the banks, about 75 percent of the banks that were members of the Federal Reserve System had been reopened. A little more than a month after the beginning of the bank holiday, member banks of the Federal Reserve System holding 90 percent of all member bank deposits had been reopened. By the beginning of April, only about 70 percent of the state-chartered banks that were ultimately to reopen had been reopened.

Roosevelt's actions at the beginning of his term were a dramatic contrast to those of his predecessor. The bank holiday seemed to restore the public's confidence in the nation's banks, and American citizens redeposited more than $1 billion that had been withdrawn and put away during the banking panic. The public continued to convert cash holdings into deposits until early 1935 while banks continued to accumulate larger amounts of excess reserves throughout the 1930s. With the end of the bank runs, bank failures quickly subsided. From 1934 through 1940 only 448 banks suspended operations, an average of just 64 each year compared to 2,294 in 1931 and 1,486 in 1932. The banking system realized its first signs of stability since 1930.

But Roosevelt did more. He moved to sever the U.S. commitment to the fixed gold value of the dollar, something that had been anathema to Hoover. The Emergency Banking Act gave Roosevelt the power to control foreign exchange transactions and gold and currency movements, options that he quickly utilized. On April 5 he issued an executive order requiring American citizens to surrender all gold certificates and gold except for rare gold coins. On April 18 he prohibited the private export of gold and indicated he would support the Thomas Amendment to the Agricultural Adjustment Act, allowing the president to set the price of gold—an action that clearly meant devaluing the dollar. The dollar then began to float and declined in value against most currencies. On June 5, Congress abrogated all gold clauses in contracts.

Finally, the Gold Reserve Act of January 1934 formalized the executive orders pertaining to gold and set the value of gold at $35 an ounce as the United States abandoned the gold coin standard. The devaluation of the dollar by nearly 70 percent tended to raise both the prices of imported goods and the prices of U.S. exports. Prices for exported farm products, primarily grains and cotton, quickly rose, boosting the incomes of cotton and grain farmers. The formal devaluation of the dollar in January 1934 initiated a golden avalanche as gold poured into the United States. Between December 1933 and July 1934 the country's monetary gold stocks swelled from $4.04 billion to $7.9 billion, an increase of 96 percent. With the rise of the Nazi party in Germany, worried Europeans continued to ship gold to the safety of the United States, and by December 1938 the monetary gold stock had reached $14.5 billion, 259 percent larger than in December 1933. This flow of gold allowed the money supply to expand despite the failure of the Board of Governors of the Federal Reserve System to take actions to expand it. In 1936, in fact, the board took steps to contract the money supply. The increase in the money

supply brought about by the inflow of gold following devaluation was one of the few forces that unambiguously worked to
expand economic activity from 1934 to 1940.

Roosevelt's commanding presence led people to believe that
positive things were happening. And they were. The bank
holiday and the reopening of the banks stabilized the banking
system. In conjunction with the devaluation of the dollar, this
signaled that deflationary policies had ended. The Federal Reserve System no longer had to take deflationary steps to defend the dollar, and, though the Federal Reserve undertook
no expansionary monetary policy, the money supply at last
stopped declining. Economic activity quickly responded to
these initiatives. Between March and July 1933 nondurable
manufacturing production increased 35 percent while durable
manufacturing production increased 83 percent. The estimated monthly unemployment rate declined from 28.3 percent in March to 23.3 percent in July. If this rate of recovery
had continued, by October 1934 the unemployment rate
would have been below 5 percent. In February 1934 durable
manufacturing production would have surpassed its July 1929
peak.

But this rapid recovery did not continue. Between July and
November 1933 there was little change in the unemployment
rate. Although it fell early in 1934, by September and October
of that year it was as high as it had been in July 1933. Durable
manufacturing production fell in September and by November was 32 percent below the July 1933 level. Nondurable
production fell 19 percent over the same period. Durable
manufacturing production again reached the July 1933 level
in May 1934 and then began declining. It recovered to a point
slightly higher than the July 1933 level in February 1935 and
remained stuck there through July. Overall manufacturing
production sank and did not reach the July 1933 level until
August 1935. By September 1933 the promising recovery of

the economy had stalled. It did not resume until the late summer of 1935.

THE FIRST HUNDRED DAYS

To explain this stall, we must first look at the other actions taken by the Roosevelt administration. During the first hundred days of the New Deal, more major legislation was enacted than ever before in so short a period. A Democratic Congress had been elected with Roosevelt, and they, as well as the president, were anxious to "do something." They quickly passed the bills that Roosevelt's advisers sent up, and just as quickly he signed them.

First came a series of acts designed to reform the financial sector and promote financial recovery. The Emergency Banking Act of March 9 was replaced by the reform-oriented Banking Act of 1933. The Federal Reserve System was directed to supervise and control all foreign transactions. Roosevelt's advisers believe that the banks' payment of interest on checking account (or demand) deposits had led them to invest these volatile deposits in riskier short-term loans. To correct this, the bill prohibited the payment of interest on checking accounts. To reduce competitive pressures among banks to pay higher interest rates to attract more deposits, the Federal Reserve System was authorized to set maximum rates that could be paid on savings and time deposits.

Roosevelt's advisers also believed that commercial banks had used volatile checking account deposits to underwrite new securities issues, and that this contributed to problems in the securities market during the crash and depression. Therefore investment and commercial banking were separated. To reduce the likelihood of further runs on banks by panicky depositors, the Federal Deposit Insurance Corporation (FDIC) was created to provide temporary insurance for deposits in

commercial banks. A similar agency, the Federal Savings and
Loan Insurance Corporation, FSLIC, was created to provide
temporary insurance for savings and time deposits in thrift institutions. The Banking Act of 1935 made the FDIC and the
FSLIC permanent. It also reorganized the Federal Reserve
System to reduce political pressures on the system's directors
and centralize authority in the Board of Governors in Washington, D.C.

To provide immediate relief for the mortgage debts of
farmers and homeowners, the Federal Farm Mortgage Corporation and the Home Owners Loan Corporation were created. These temporary institutions provided credit to stave off
foreclosures, postpone payments, and scale down debts. Federal banks to provide short-term and long-term credit for the
agricultural sector were created as well as new federal banks
to provide credit to the Savings and Loan Associations that
provided the bulk of home mortgage credit.

Other measures were directed more toward reform. On
May 27, 1933, Congress passed the Securities Act to begin re-
forming and regulating the securities markets. The Securities
and Exchange Act of June 6, 1934, created the Securities and
Exchange Commission (SEC), to oversee the nation's securities exchanges, set rules by which securities were issued, marketed, and sold, and gave the Federal Reserve System the
power to set margin requirements on securities purchases.

The reform measures also extended to utilities. While governor of New York, Roosevelt had favored public-owned electric utilities over those that were private and investor-owned.
Arguing that the federal government's 1920s investment in
flood control and navigation in the Muscle Shoals area of the
Tennessee River had not been utilized, Roosevelt asked Congress on April 10, 1933, to establish the Tennessee Valley Authority to build dams that would harness the river's nearly
annual floods while supplying electricity to the region. The

TVA would also provide a yardstick by which to measure the performance of the private, investor-owned electric utilities and to determine their regulation.

With the massive unemployment that existed in 1933, many families depended on government relief. Some estimates suggested that 10 percent of the nation's families relied on relief, with one-third of these in the northern states of New York, Pennsylvania, Ohio, and Illinois. To provide immediate relief to these beleaguered citizens, Congress on May 12, 1933, passed the Federal Emergency Relief Act. Direct federal money grants went to states that would provide additional funds from their own treasuries. The FERA also established a number of programs to provide work relief. These included the Civil Works Service Program, the Emergency Education Program, and the Women's Work Program. The Civilian Conservation Corps, another work relief program passed in this early period, continued through the 1930s. It aimed to develop young men through hard work in forests and national parks while simultaneously conserving resources.

Driven by the arguments of Harry Hopkins, the administration concluded that these efforts would not be sufficient as the winter of 1933–1934 approached. It asked for, and Congress passed, the temporary Civil Works Administration (CWA) to provide immediate employment to four million unemployed workers. Hopkins ordered his staff to come up with whatever jobs they could quickly dream up to get the money out to those in need; as a consequence he received extensive criticism for his "wasteful" expenditures. The program was quickly dismantled in the spring of 1934, and the FERA reassumed the major burden of relief. Although the FERA combined direct and work relief, both Roosevelt and Hopkins believed that direct relief tended to be psychologically debilitating, weakening and even destroying the will to provide for oneself. They preferred work relief in which recipients "earned" what they received. They also concluded that if direct relief had to be provided, it was best administered by state and local governments that were more familiar with the needs of their unemployed. As a result, in 1935 the FERA was replaced with the Works Progress Administration (WPA). The WPA developed local public works construction projects as well as other projects designed to employ local writers and artists.

THE FIRST AGRICULTURAL ADJUSTMENT ACT

The centerpieces of Roosevelt's early New Deal efforts in 1933 were the Agricultural Adjustment Act (AAA) of May 12 and the National Industrial Recovery Act (NIRA) of June 16. The authors of the AAA intended to reform American agriculture in order to bring relief to the nation's farmers; it set in motion programs whose descendants exist today. Farmers had long been unhappy with agricultural markets. Many believed they were too volatile and had a tendency toward lower and lower prices that were depriving farmers of their rightful income and reducing their status in society. During the 1920s several corrective bills—a dual price system with lower export prices; McNary-Haugen plans to raise prices to target levels; and a plan to reduce production and guarantee prices through production allotments—were proposed but never enacted, or were vetoed by the president. The objective of these plans was to fix prices, thereby reducing price instability and raising prices for farmers.

The AAA introduced the use of "parity" prices, intended to give farmers the same purchasing power they had enjoyed in the "golden" years of 1910–1914. To do this, commodity prices were to be raised relative to the cost of farm inputs until they achieved the same ratio as in the earlier period. The current price that would equalize these ratios was the "parity" price.

Initially only wheat, cotton, field corn, rice, tobacco, milk and milk products, and hogs were subject to parity prices. The list of "basic" commodities was expanded in 1934 and 1935 to include rye, flax, barley, grain sorghums, cattle, sugar beets, sugar cane, and potatoes.

The AAA provided several mechanisms for achieving parity prices. These included production controls, benefit payments, nonrecourse loans, and marketing agreements. If a farmer agreed to limit production he was given benefit payments derived from taxes levied on the primary (or first) processors of the agricultural produce. Most of this tax would then be passed on to consumers, so the prices of food and cotton clothing would rise because of the reduced supply and because of the processing tax. With the buyers of agricultural produce relatively insensitive to the prices they paid for the produce, small declines in production would result in relatively large increases in prices, leading to a growth in farm incomes. To help in reducing production and raising prices, the Department of Agriculture would also use nonrecourse loans from the Commodity Credit Corporation (CCC). Under this loan program, a farmer received a loan from the CCC equal to the target price for each unit (bushel, pound, bale, etc.) of the commodity produced under the production agreement the farmer had signed. If the market price failed to rise to the target price the farmer simply defaulted on the loan and the CCC took ownership of the commodity. If the market price rose above the target price, the farmer could sell the commodity on the open market and pay off the loan from proceeds of the sale.

Marketing agreements suspended the anti-trust laws for buyers of the commodities, allowing them to set target prices at which they agreed to buy. The Agriculture Department agreed to buy, at the target price, any commodities that the processors could not sell at that price. This was the primary mechanism by which the prices of milk and milk products were raised. It was also used by some states, such as California and Arizona, to raise prices. A marketing board was established to determine how much of a fresh fruit (for example, oranges or lemons) or a fresh vegetable should be marketed in order to achieve a target price. Marketing quotas were then issued to the farmers telling them how much they could send to market. Production in excess of their marketing quota had to be destroyed or sent to a secondary market, such as those for frozen orange juice or lemon juice.

Roosevelt wanted the farm program to be voluntary and its administration to be decentralized so that farmers themselves would determine its direction and magnitude—a "grass-roots democracy." But a number of farmers were quite willing to use coercive measures to be certain that all farmers cooperated, and their calls led to some agricultural legislation that provided mandates. The Bankhead cotton control bill of 1934, designed to reduce cotton production and raise cotton prices, allowed the government to levy a tax on a producer which could equal 50 percent of the current price on cotton produced in excess of the farmer's quota. The Kerr-Smith Tobacco Act of 1934 required that tobacco produced in excess of a farmer's quota could be taxed at a rate equal to one-third of its average selling price. The results of the decentralization experiment were little better. Rather than most local farmers joining in a committee or association to make production decisions, it was generally the largest, wealthiest farmers, the Farm Bureau, and the Extension Service that wielded power and made decisions.

Two early AAA programs caused considerable controversy. Surveys in the spring of 1933 led AAA officials to conclude that the large numbers of young pigs and the extent of cotton plantings would increase the supply of pork and cotton, driving down their prices still further. The AAA therefore undertook to have six million baby pigs slaughtered and to persuade farmers to sell off some breeding sows to relief programs and fertilizer producers. To reduce cotton production the AAA paid farmers eleven dollars an acre to plow up one-fourth of the forty million acres of cotton already planted. Although the payments were intended for the cotton farmers, including tenants and sharecroppers, in many cases they went to the landowners; the tenants and sharecroppers receiving nothing.

The Agricultural Adjustment Act of 1933 was not thought of as a long-term solution to the farm problem, nor did it embody radically new ideas. The component parts had been proposed before, particularly in the 1920s, but not put into practice. Although the first AAA did direct additional funds toward farmers, and the improvement in the economy had some effect in increasing demand, the primary factors that brought higher farm prices were natural forces. Droughts had been a periodic problem in the Midwest and Plains states and had reappeared in 1930. In 1934 and again in 1936 droughts afflicted huge areas of these regions as well as some Southern areas. Great dust storms appeared in the Southern Plains states, though these were in fact nothing new. The production of many commodities declined—for example, the United States, usually an exporter of wheat, imported wheat in 1934 and 1936—and commodity prices rose. The price of a bushel of corn increased from 32 cents a bushel in 1932 to 52 cents in 1933, 84 cents in 1934, and $1.04 in 1936 as production declined. Wheat prices behaved similarly, rising from 38 cents a bushel in 1932 to 74 cents, 85 cents, and finally to $1.02 in 1936. Prices for cotton, rice, barley, sorghum, oats, peanuts, hay, potatoes, and other commodities also rose.

Because of reduced production due to the droughts, the Agriculture Department initially did not have to purchase many surplus commodities in order to maintain higher support prices. But higher prices did little to help drought-stricken farmers who had little to sell. The first Agricultural Adjustment Act was of relatively little help to these farmers. Like later agricultural acts in the 1930s—the Soil Conservation and Domestic Allotment Act and the Second Agricultural Adjustment Act—and post–World War II programs, the AAA primarily helped larger, wealthier farmers, not small, impoverished farmers who really needed help. It was essentially a program to transfer income from nonfarmers to farmers. By the late 1930s government stores of surplus commodities were growing alarmingly. The problem of government purchases of what would otherwise be surplus commodities continued to plague agricultural programs in the postwar years.

THE NATIONAL INDUSTRIAL RECOVERY ACT

The second cornerstone of Roosevelt's early New Deal was the National Industrial Recovery Act. Title I of the act established the National Recovery Administration (NRA) while Title II established the Public Works Administration (PWA). Harold Ickes, secretary of the interior, supervised the PWA, which was intended as a combination of relief through public employment and a program to create needed public infrastructure. During its life the PWA built highways and public buildings, improved harbors, funded the construction of municipal power plants, and undertook the construction of dams, including the Bonneville and Grand Coulee dams on the Columbia River. Ickes's approach to the PWA was in conflict with some of the objectives of the work relief project. He preferred to go slow to make certain that all projects were economically worthwhile and that expenditures were not wasted. He preferred to use more capital equipment and materials, and less manpower, to reduce costs. He also wanted to be certain that the men he hired had the necessary skills rather than hiring just anyone who was on relief or was unemployed. As a result, the PWA was slow in getting started and had less of an impact than its designers had envisioned.

The National Recovery Administration was conceived as an alternative to a maximum-hours bill proposed by Senator Hugo Black of Alabama. On April 6, 1933, the Senate passed Black's thirty-hour bill that would have prohibited the interstate shipment of goods produced by employees who worked more than six hours a day or five days a week. This bill reflected the popular notion that the way to confront the depression was to spread the available work among more workers by legislating a reduction of the workweek. President Roosevelt believed that the bill, as written, was unconstitutional, but he did not wish to veto a bill that Democratic lawmakers had sent him. So he asked Frances Perkins, the secretary of labor, to devise an alternative bill. Perkins's alternative suggestion was to institute minimum wages with possible limitations on machine-hours and hours of work per week. Other groups were working on bills with similar intentions of easing the depression in the industrial sector.

The proposals that coalesced into the National Recovery Administration tended to reflect what many individuals in the administration believed was a major reason for the Great Depression—"underconsumption" or "overproduction." Some believed that the nation's industrial production had grown faster than consumer demand, leading to excessive quantities of durable goods such as automobiles, housing, and large household appliances. And the wages of the typical production worker had not grown as fast as his productivity. This left too much income in the hands of the wealthy, encouraging savings relative to consumption. The Roosevelt administration's solution to this fundamental problem of underconsumption was to reduce production and increase the incomes of the workers who consumed more and saved less. Such changes required the reform of industrial activity. Most of those who wrote what became the NIRA believed that the United States could not forgo the advantages offered by big businesses. The problem was to harness or reform them.

For example, Raymond Moley wanted to establish national planning based on the model of the War Industries Board of World War I, where businesses jointly cooperated with government in developing their plans. Moley invited General Hugh Johnson, who had been the military's representative to the WIB during the war, to assist him, and together they proposed to suspend the anti-trust laws, have the president sanction business agreements on competitiveness and labor practices, and institute federal licensing to secure the agreement of firms. John Dickinson, Jerome Frank, and Rexford Tugwell were working on a bill that would have used trade associations, which had mushroomed during the 1920s, as instruments of national planning. These advisers had little confidence that a competitive market system could coordinate economic activities and restore full employment in the economy. They pushed for government officials to be the controlling voices in business planning and were considered to be among the more "radical" planners. Senator Robert Wagner of New York was preparing a bill authorizing public works, direct loans to industry, and government-sanctioned trade association agreements as a means of recovery.

These different groups came together to compromise and write the bill that created the National Recovery Administration. The NRA authorized firms to write codes of fair competition for their industry, which they would then honor in their daily operations. Industry trade associations would be the primary vehicles through which this program was accomplished. The codes of fair competition would be sanctioned by the federal government and could be legally enforced on the firms through an exemption from the anti-trust laws. The act also included minimum labor standards which included the elimination of child labor and sweatshops, adequate or acceptable maximum hours and minimum wages, and desirable working conditions, though these were not carefully defined. At Senator Wagner's insistence, a section was added—Section 7a—which required firms to recognize and bargain with labor unions democratically chosen by a firm's employees, and forbade yellow dog contracts (stating that employees would not join a union). This collective bargaining was to be overseen by a National Labor Board. The NRA was authorized to operate for two years, at which time it would be reassessed.

The NRA drew upon a number of different ideas and developments in vogue at the time. Some businessmen believed that overproduction could be eliminated through such tactics as production quotas, price agreements, entry controls (to regulate the entry of new firms into a market), and cost-accounting formulas to calculate the correct economic price. These measures could eliminate unfair price-cutting and promote stability. They fit in with, and could be used by, intellectuals who believed that the United States should move to a collectivist democracy that used purposeful national planning. The planning, as envisioned by Moley and other moderates, would be undertaken jointly through the participation of business, labor, consumer groups, and the government. In the view of Tugwell and more radical planners, the "technocrats"—technicians, economists, engineers, and other experts—would play a major role by providing advice to the government officials who would direct the planning. In this way waste could be eliminated and production directed to maximize the widespread benefits of society rather than primarily aimed at enhancing the wealth and power of those who controlled businesses in the economy.

The NRA established three boards to advise General Johnson, appointed by Roosevelt the NRA's administrator. These were an Industrial Advisory Board, a Labor Advisory Board, and a Consumers' Advisory Board. In practice, the Labor and Consumers' advisory boards had little influence. A deputy administrator was appointed for each industry to supervise code writing. These administrators were usually drawn from firms in the industry or from affiliated organizations such as a trade association, or from the military. The code writing committees were similarly drawn largely from trade associations and firms in the industry, in line with Johnson's desire to see the NRA be an exercise in industrial self-government. The codes also named authorities who would administer and enforce the codes. Not surprisingly, representatives of the firms in the industry also dominated these authorities. Less than 10 percent of the authorities included labor representatives, and less than 2 percent included consumer representatives.

Some common themes could be found among the industry codes. Firms generally wished to raise prices and bring stability to their industries. Thus most of the codes contained minimum-price provisions to reduce price-cutting by "chiselers," as they were often called. Few codes were able to employ direct price controls, but prohibiting sales below cost (however defined) was aimed at the same thing. To be certain that firms did not cheat by manipulating their cost calculations, the codes proposed the development of uniform cost-accounting formulas. In some cases when this was difficult, code authorities simply specified standard production costs, without research into the member firms' costs. At the retail level, minimum markups were proposed as well as resale price maintenance—where firms agreed to sell at retail prices suggested by the manufacturers. This aimed not only to eliminate price-cutting but to preserve existing distribution systems using wholesalers and jobbers, by reducing the advantages of the chain stores. Prices could be stabilized and price-cutting stopped through open-price systems where businesses filed their prices and then openly exchanged their price statistics with others, especially their competitors. Some codes required the filing of past as well as current prices, and many required waiting periods before prices could be changed after the filing of a price change. This made it easier to bring pressures to bear on firms proposing price cuts. Standardizing sales practices and nonprice competition—such as combination sales, trade-in allowances, and credit terms—could further reduce competition. To help preserve existing distribution channels and combat chain stores, codes restricted quantity discounts, advertising allowances, and brokerage fees.

Prices could also be supported by controlling production. In this way firms would not have an incentive to reduce prices to sell their surplus production. Thus codes sometimes included limits on the hours a machine or a plant could be operated, direct production quotas, provisions for inventory control, and restrictions on the construction of new plants, reopening of closed plants, or expansion of existing plants. For example, in industries where machine production could be more easily measured—textiles, glass containers, canning and packing, for instance—codes limited the hours per day or week machines or plants could be operated. Maximum production quotas were common in commercial fishing, iron and steel, copper, cement, and crude oil industries. The codes sometimes discouraged the production of different product lines in order to reduce investment. Initially the codes drawn up by the industries contained little about fair labor practices, such as wages, hours, working conditions, and collective bargaining.

Once a code was approved by the NRA, it attained the force of law and was binding on all the firms in the industry, whether or not they had signed an NRA agreement. Code authorities could resort to the courts for enforcement, but in practice this was infrequent.

Once Roosevelt approved the NRA on June 16, 1933, industries began to develop codes quickly. By July 27, 209 national industry codes had been submitted. But this was too slow for General Johnson and the president, even though the NRA was becoming bogged down in the approval process. As a result, Roosevelt and Johnson began a nationwide campaign to persuade firms and industries to sign a "blanket" code while their industries proceeded to draw up a code for submission. Most signed the blanket agreement, allowing them to display the blue eagle insignia indicating that they supported the NRA. The blanket code tended to place more emphasis on shortening the workweek to spread the work, stabilizing or raising wages, and minimizing price increases. It helped spur industries to write their own codes for submission to the NRA. By May 1935 it was estimated that 95 percent of all industrial workers were covered by NRA codes.

THE RECOVERY FROM 1933 TO 1935

General Johnson initiated a huge nationwide publicity campaign for the NRA as soon as Roosevelt signed it into law on June 16, 1933. Johnson argued that it was unpatriotic for a firm to ignore NRA provisions and for an individual to patronize any business that did not display the blue eagle insignia indicating NRA support. Only in this manner, Johnson and Roosevelt argued, was it possible for the nation to engage in the great cooperative effort necessary to reemploy workers, shorten the workweek, pay a "decent" wage, and prevent the unfair competition and overproduction that had helped bring on the depression. If a firm displayed the blue eagle it was to be taken as a sign that this firm was doing its duty to help bring the nation out of the devastating contraction. Both within the government and among firms and the general population, Johnson's publicity campaign aroused high expectations that this, indeed, was the initiative that could pull the American economy out of the depression.

At first it appeared that Americans' expectations would be realized. Industrial production rose quickly and unemployment fell from March through July 1933—but these optimistic signs did not last. The indexes show that industrial production began to fall and continued to fall to the end of 1933. A significant part of the March to July gains were lost in the last five months of 1933, and the unemployment rate stopped falling. Some of the air in the inflated expectations of the NRA began to leak out by late 1933 and early 1934 as problems with the agency began to surface.

The self-government by industries that General Johnson had aimed for turned out differently in practice. Generally the large firms in an industry dominated the code authorities and promulgated rules and actions that tended to favor, not surprisingly, the largest firms. Critics commonly charged that the NRA had fostered the cartelization of many industries because of the lack of effective labor, consumer, and government representation. Neither those who preferred small independent businesses—the anti-trusters associated with Supreme Court Justice Louis Brandeis and law professor Felix Frankfurter—nor those who advocated effective national planning—whether through cooperation with big business (such as Raymond Moley) or through the harnessing of big business (such as Rexford Tugwell)—were happy with what they saw. The planners believed that the opportunity for national planning was slipping away as the NRA ceded control to firms within industries. The anti-trusters saw the growth of monopolies. Most codes employed rules to raise prices, hold down wages, and stop competition within the industry, and the anti-trusters saw this as evidence of the growth of government-fostered cartels.

Labor leaders were no happier. Although American Federation of Labor (AFL) unions had made gains in organizing labor, they felt that the NRA's labor agenda had been twisted. An early ruling gave firms the right to organize company-dominated labor unions to represent their employees. Thus independent unions, essentially those affiliated with the AFL, had not realized the gains some thought they should have made. Even within the labor movement there was growing dissension. The old-line skilled craft unions of the AFL were, at best, ambivalent about organizing industrial unions that cut across craft lines, whose workers were relatively unskilled, and whose numbers might overwhelm the smaller, more elite, craft unions. By moving cautiously in many cases, the AFL had allowed firms to surge ahead with company unions when there was a strike or strike threat, or when an AFL-affiliated union had made headway in a plant. By mid-1934 more than one-fourth of all industrial workers were employed in plants that had company unions, and about two-thirds of those unions were established after the NRA was enacted.

Conflicts within industries were also developing. It was sometimes difficult to classify firms into an industry. Firms often produced a variety of products that were in several different industry classifications, and the codes were not consistent across industries. To put all competitors on the same footing, the codes generally required that all firms pay the same wages and charge the same prices. Firms argued over appropriate wage rates and wage differentials for traditional skilled labor. Some firms—usually younger, growing enterprises—resisted production controls. Finally, increases in wholesale and retail prices and in industrial wages began to be generally noticed and criticized by many consumer organizations, government officials, the press, and others.

The price provisions of the codes never achieved universal compliance, and this situation worsened over time. By May

1934 compliance among barbers, beauticians, and dry cleaners had almost completely broken down. In general, maintaining and enforcing the codes was more difficult in industries where most of the firms produced unstandardized products and where entry was easier. It was also difficult for the NRA to bring about cooperation, in particular to stop price cheating, in markets that were larger and growing, where simple technologies were employed, or where one group wanted to use the codes to gain a competitive advantage over another group. The lumber industry was a good example of this as well as almost all retail and service trades. It was also difficult to monitor the complex structure of prices in most industries—there were different types and sizes of products, different classes of buyers, widely varying locations of buyers and sellers, and other complexities. As a result it was difficult to detect price cheating, and even when detected, to punish it. The ultimate and only truly effective control was prosecution in the courts, but the NRA did not often pursue such prosecution. This was partly due to the NRA's philosophy of self-regulation and partly due to growing doubts about its constitutionality.

The NRA, as it was created and it evolved, failed to satisfy the anti-trusters or the planners. General Johnson had a difficult time handling criticism of the agency and resisted attempts to meddle with it. Finally he began to respond. In a memo of June 7, 1934, he acknowledged the anti-trusters' criticisms and declared that the NRA's goal was free markets and strengthened competition. In response to the subsequent business outcry, he qualified the memo to apply only to future NRA codes, not the current codes—which, of course, meant that principles of competition had little effect because nearly all industries already had NRA codes. Under pressure from all sides, and losing Roosevelt's confidence, Johnson resigned on August 21, 1934. Roosevelt then reorganized the leadership of the NRA by creating a five-man National Industrial Recovery Board, but this new board largely embodied the existing stalemate within the NRA and was no better in providing leadership and effective action.

Many critics might have been willing to overlook these problems if the NRA had brought about the recovery that Roosevelt and Johnson had promised. But this was not the case. By the end of 1934 the unemployment rate was as high as it had been in July 1933. Through most of 1935, unemployment averaged about 20 percent. Estimates of the number of workers unemployed that were reported to newspapers showed little decline since the summer of 1933. Industrial production, particularly durable manufacturing production, showed similar trends and did not finally begin to rise until after July 1935. Nondurable manufacturing behaved in much the same way, showing no evidence of sustained recovery before the last half of 1935. Indexes of business activity compiled by the *New York Times,* the *New York Herald-Tribune,* and other newspapers and private organizations reported even poorer economic performance over the course of the NRA. Critics also noted the rising prices and wage rates and falling hours in the workweek. As disillusionment with the NRA spread, the administration encountered a growing unwillingness to continue to tolerate the New Deal's experiment in industrial planning.

WHY WAS THE RECOVERY FROM 1933 TO 1935 SO SLOW?

Although the word "recovery" is in the title of the National Recovery Administration, there has been continued debate over its primary emphasis. Was it to bring recovery or reform to the industrial sector? The NRA was a hastily thrown together bill that suffered from internal contradictions and was inconsistent with other New Deal programs. There were continuing arguments over what the NRA really meant and how it was to be put into practice. None of the groups who were party to its creation were really happy with the resulting bill.

Moley, Johnson, and more moderate planners wanted national industrial planning by representatives of all relevant interests in the society—plannng that was coordinated by the wise and impartial hands of government representatives. In this way the potential of big business organizations could be harnessed for the benefit of everyone in the society. The more radical planners, such as Tugwell, Frank, and Dickinson, who had little confidence in a competitive market system, wanted government actively to direct the planning. Planners like Tugwell were not the least bit worried by the potential loss of freedom this could entail. Business interests, on the other hand, wanted relief from the anti-trust laws so that they could be allowed to reduce what they called "cutthroat" pricing and excessive production and bring order to the chaos of competitive markets. Senator Wagner and Secretary of Labor Perkins wanted to improve the status and well-being of workers through legislation and the organization of labor unions. There is little evidence that recovery was first on the agenda of any of these competing groups; rather, all intended first to reform industry in one way or another, in order to move to the "correct" path of recovery.

No group received what it really wanted. Businesses obtained relief (albeit temporary) from anti-trust laws but were supposed to share planning with labor and consumer representatives while being supervised by the government. Planning tended to be dominated by business interests and was not coordinated within and between industries as the planners wanted. Workers found that company unions and business intransigence kept them from achieving the gains they sought. The result was a frustrating mess that became worse as the months passed.

The key to the NRA's success was the set of industrial codes of fair competition that all firms in every industry were supposed to observe. In the spirit of industrial self-government, each industry was to write its own codes, taking care, of course, to consider labor and the consumer in the process. In practice, the responsibility was usually delegated to the industry's trade association, if there was such a body. The first code approved by the NRA, on July 9, 1933, was the Cotton Textile Code. The universal temporary code (called the President's Reemployment Agreements) were launched in July 1933, and by early September more than 2.3 million firms employing over 16 million workers had agreed to the PRAs. They were replaced by industry codes as these were drawn up and approved, and by May 1935, when the NRA ended because of a Supreme Court ruling, 557 national industry codes had been approved.

A comparison of the PRAs and typical industry codes indicates some of the problems with the NRA. The PRAs were strong on labor and wage commandments. Firms were not to employ child labor. White-collar workers were not to work more than forty hours a week and were to be paid at least twelve to fifteen dollars a week, depending on the size of the city where the firm was located. Blue-collar workers were to work no more than eight hours a day and thirty-five hours a week, with a minimum wage rate of forty cents an hour or the wage rate prevailing on July 25, 1929, if that was lower—but in no case could the wage rate be less than thirty cents an hour. Wage rates were not to be reduced and were to be raised where necessary for a fair wage structure. Prices were not to be raised above the level prevailing on July 1, 1933, unless it could be shown that cost increases justified an increase. The codes stated explicitly that the objective was to shorten the hours worked each week—in order to spread the available work—and to raise the wages on the shorter workweek to a living basis. These price and wage commandments bordered on the irrational. Prices and wage rates had fallen significantly in the deflation between 1929 and 1933, and few firms had shown profits during the last three years of the contraction. Yet firms were expected to raise wage rates to a level that was at or near wage rates in 1929 while keeping prices at the level of the summer of 1933—and at the same time they were to reduce the workweek to spread the work.

The codes drawn up by the industries had quite different orientations. Roosevelt's critics commonly charged that the NRA was creating monopolies. In retrospect the NRA can be seen as a massive U.S. experiment with government-sponsored cartelization. In a cartel the firms in an industry band together to reduce (or eliminate) competition in the industry. The firms set similar, if not uniform, prices and then together raise prices and reduce production to maximize the industry's profits. At times this involves reducing the industry's production capacity, and almost always it requires halting any expansion in the industry's capacity through a member firm's expansion or through the entry of new firms. Granted an exemption from the anti-trust laws and pushed hard by the federal government to form cartels, the industrial firms responded as one would expect them to respond. They attempted to raise prices, stop price-cutting, and reduce production in order to restore profitability. Nearly every industry code attempted to specify the minimum prices at which the industry's products should be sold, and then it set out conditions to increase the minimum price so that it would become the prevailing price. To make the higher prices effective, production had to be controlled. Greater production would pressure firms into cutting prices to sell the increased output.

Thus the NRA was attuned to discourage recovery, and that is exactly what it did. By September 1933 the NRA codes were taking effect; consistent with their emphasis, production declined between August and November. Factory employment, which had been increasing until September, began falling and continued to fall into January 1934. Wholesale prices rose 12 percent between June and December 1933, after which the rate of increase slowed sharply. Nominal factory wage rates in twenty-five manufacturing industries had fallen through June 1933; for the two months from July to September, wage rates increased by 19 percent as firms adopted the NRA blanket code. The rate of increase then slowed somewhat, and by May 1934 money wage rates had risen another 9.5 percent from September 1933, and real wage rates had increased 23.1 percent from July 1933. By that time many industries had finished formulating their specific industry codes. For the next fourteen months, May 1934 to July 1935, the average money wage rate in these twenty-five manufacturing industries increased only 2.4 percent, and the real wage rate fell 2.7 percent.

The NRA had achieved at least some of its objectives. It had increased real and nominal wage rates, primarily in one large jump between July 1933 and September 1933, as a means of fighting "underconsumption." It was also successful in spreading the work by reducing the number of hours worked for a typical worker. But advocates of independent labor unions watched in horror as company unions arose to neutralize the independent power of workers. Recovery, measured by increasing production and resource employment, largely ceased during the life of the NRA, nor did the NRA initiate a new era of stability through centralized planning. The dissension and confusion in nearly all the industries governed by NRA codes grew worse in 1934 and 1935.

Disagreements between firms quickly developed. They disagreed on prevailing prices and wage rates and wage rate differentials, on product standards, on production quotas, and on market shares. Labor disputes were widespread. Smaller firms that had found a market niche through lower prices often produced their goods outside of urban areas and paid lower wage rates. Code authorities, dominated by the larger firms in the industry, pressed for uniform hourly wage rates—which reduced smaller firms' advantages. Uniform prices too often worked to the disadvantage of smaller producers. For example, smaller, off-brand tire producers complained bitterly that uniform prices for various types and sizes of tires reduced their ability to compete with national brand tires from larger producers. Complaints of this sort were common and were to be expected when large firms dominated in drawing up codes.

Assigning firms to industries covered by codes also presented difficulties, particularly when a firm produced an array of products. Some industry codes were broad—those for structural steel, for example—while others were quite narrow, such as those for artificial limbs, city directories, shoulder pads, bouillon cubes, and corset steel. The multiplication of industry codes reinforced rather than resolved intra-industry disputes and complicated life for integrated firms. Writing codes for large industries dominated by fewer firms was easier; writing codes for smaller, more competitive industries with numerous producers, often geographically dispersed, was quite difficult. Some smaller industries dragged out this process and were not yet covered by codes when the NRA was declared unconstitutional.

Policing the codes was difficult and in some cases nearly impossible. Honest reporting by firms was not the norm. Integrated producers were often able to shuffle costs between products and divisions and were able to increase profits because of access to competitors' prices. Within a short time cheating on prices became common, especially in the smaller,

more competitive industries where policing was more difficult. When price-cutting, wage rates below code, or other
types of cheating were discovered, they were often not prose-
cuted.

All the initiatives created under the "enlightened management" of the NRA were inimical to recovery. The American
economy had contracted—production had declined because of
a general decline in demand. The depression had occurred not
because of the production of excessive amounts of most goods.
It was not the case that business and consumer demands were
saturated. Rather, recovery required restoring demands for investment and consumer goods and reemploying the resources
that had been idled by the contraction. But this was not the in-
tention of the NRA codes. Producers were expected to increase prices and hold the line on or reduce production so as to
restore profitability—exactly the opposite of what recovery required. Growing disagreements over the rules and growing
noncompliance with them created uncertainty and confusion,
discouraging firms from taking actions that might have increased production or investments that might have given
them competitive advantages. Thus during the life of the
NRA, the recovery from the Great Depression largely stalled.

The goals of these early New Deal programs were inconsistent. Manufacturers, distributors, and retailers wanted higher
prices relative to costs so that they could increase profits.
Workers wanted rising wage rates relative to prices, in order
to increase real wages. Increases in the price of manufactured
products increased farmers' costs, reducing their real incomes,
but the AAA sought rising prices for farm products, relative
to the price of manufactured products, in order to raise farmers' real incomes. Only by increasing productivity in industry
and farming could real incomes and profits rise everywhere,
but productivity enhancements were a minor component of

AAA policies and for the most part were ignored in NRA codes and policies.

THE END OF THE NRA

In the late spring of 1935, Roosevelt was preparing to confront criticisms of the NRA and falling support for the agency as he prepared to ask Congress to extend its life. The Supreme Court took the issue out of his hands. On May 27, 1935, in the *Schecter* case, the Court unanimously ruled the NRA unconstitutional. The case had begun in 1934 when the Justice Department concluded that the A. L. A. Schecter Poultry Corporation had violated the live poultry code in supplying Jewish residents in Brooklyn with kosher poultry. The eighteen counts against the firm included a single count of selling a single "unfit" chicken to a butcher, two counts of violating the maximum-hour and minimum-wage provisions of the NRA live poultry code, and two counts of inaccurate reporting. Ten of the counts charged that the firm allowed customers to choose the chickens they wanted to purchase rather than taking the run of the coop. The NRA live poultry code dictated that a firm could not engage in selective killing for a customer; this was Schecter's major offense.

The administration unwisely decided to make this a test case before the Supreme Court. The Court held that the NRA was an unconstitutional delegation of legislative power and involved a situation that was not interstate commerce and not subject to federal regulation. Roosevelt was incensed at the decision and at a press conference suggested that it pushed the United States back to a horse-and-buggy definition of interstate commerce and might well bring on an economic collapse.

Further confirmation of the failure of early New Deal initiatives came on January 6, 1936, when the Court ruled in the Hoosac Mills case that the Agricultural Adjustment Act was unconstitutional. It held that the tax on processors was not simply an expropriation of money from one group for the benefit of another but invaded the reserved powers of the states because it was aimed at controlling farm production, and farm production was intrastate, not interstate, commerce.

When the Supreme Court ruled the NRA unconstitutional, there were already questions about how or if the NRA legislation would be extended. Although Roosevelt could have attempted to modify the NRA to meet the Court's objections, he chose to disband, at least temporarily, the entire structure. Privately he expected business to be in such disarray that it would initiate a call for a new NRA.

Some business leaders publicly mourned the passing of the NRA. But, released from the shackles and confusion of the NRA, businesses began increasing production. Although delayed for two years by the NRA, the recovery from the Great Depression of 1929–1933 was finally under way.

4

The Recovery Aborted, 1935–1939

THE RECOVERY of the American economy from the Great Depression finally began in the late summer of 1935. As the months passed the pace of recovery seemed to quicken, and more and more Americans began to hope that their country was returning to a more normal state. Although the Supreme Court had dealt a severe blow to the hopes of administration planners, other advisers were urging Roosevelt to change his tactics to break up big business and the concentration of wealth. As the president listened more closely to these advisers, a second New Deal took shape. By the beginning of 1937 there was a growing sense of optimism in the administration that the corner had been turned. All the indexes showed that the recovery was strengthening. Stock prices were finally rising, and unemployment appeared to be falling. With additional tax revenues from the new taxes that had been enacted and from the rising level of business activity, Roosevelt contemplated spending reductions in order to balance the federal budget. The world, indeed, seemed almost rosy at the start of 1937.

The Recovery from 1935 to 1937

In response to the *Schecter* decision, Roosevelt reduced the NRA to a minor bureau to collect statistics. He expected business activity to decline with the cessation of the NRA and for business then to call for a new NRA. What happened was the opposite. By August it was clear that business activity was increasing, not slowing, and it continued to rise and unemployment to fall until May 1937. The long-awaited recovery was finally occurring without the benefit of the NRA.

Released from the shackles of the NRA, American producers and consumers combined to initiate a real recovery. Between August 1935 and May 1937 factory employment in 25 manufacturing industries increased 24.4 percent. The unemployment rate in July 1935 was 21.3 percent, little changed from the rate of 23.3 percent in July 1933. It changed little between July and October 1935 but then began to fall. In the 14 months between October 1935 and December 1936 the unemployment rate fell from 21.9 percent to 15.3 percent. By May 1937 it had fallen to 12.3 percent. Production increased more rapidly. Nondurable manufacturing production rose 24.8 percent in the 19 months between May 1935 and December 1936 and increased another 2.4 percent by May 1937. Durable manufacturing production increased even faster, rising 49.3 percent in the 19 months between May 1935 and December 1936 and then increasing another 5.9 percent by May 1937. Stock prices also rose as the Standard and Poor's 500 industrial stock price index rose from 86 in May 1935 to 138 in May 1937.

Roosevelt Swings to the Left

Although Roosevelt could have been expected to be happy about these developments, that was not the case. The president was angry about growing criticism of his programs from business. And he was further outraged by the series of Supreme Court decisions that went against his New Deal. In January 1935 the Court had ruled against the NRA's oil industry rules. In May, just before the *Schecter* ruling, the Railroad Retirement Act had been ruled unconstitutional. As the case considering Roosevelt's abrogation of gold clauses in contracts came to the Court, he proposed to Secretary of the Treasury Morgenthau that the Treasury take steps to throw the government bond market and the foreign exchange market into turmoil. He hoped this might affect public opinion and the judiciary and result in a favorable ruling or a political setting more favorable to federal actions to control the Supreme Court. With advice from Harvard law professor Felix Frankfurter, Roosevelt began considering a constitutional amendment broadening the power of the federal government as a way around the Court.

The result was to heighten the influence of those among his advisers who were calling for an attack on the concentration of wealth and on big business. They were protégés of Frankfurter.

Frankfurter and Supreme Court Justice Louis Brandeis held similar views on the importance of small independent businesses and the federal government's role in restoring and maintaining this idyllic vision. Even before the invalidation of the NRA, Roosevelt had been influenced by the Brandeis/Frankfurter anti-trusters. Several of Frankfurter's students— Benjamin Cohen, Thomas Corcoran, and James Landis—had been instrumental in writing the new securities and banking laws. Generally these aimed at reducing the concentration of power by mandating the full disclosure of information, outlawing many securities market practices, separating investment and commercial banking, and controlling the power of the New York Federal Reserve Bank (and therefore of the

New York commercial banks) on Federal Reserve decisions. Now sensing a greater opening, the anti-trusters pushed harder on an agenda designed to restore a competitive society of small independent businesses. The attack on wealth was under way.

One of the leaders of this group was Robert Jackson, a successful upstate New York lawyer, who was brought in to revitalize the Justice Department's anti-trust division. In 1938, Roosevelt appointed him solicitor general, and in 1941 he was named to the Supreme Court. When Jackson left the anti-trust division, Roosevelt named Yale Law School professor Thurman Arnold to head the division and further expand anti-trust investigations. William O. Douglas was brought from the Yale Law School to the Securities and Exchange Commission and eventually became its chairman. Leon Henderson had joined the NRA as the consumer representative and had been a vocal opponent of the monopolization by big business that he saw there. He later joined the Securities and Exchange Commission and headed the Office of Price Administration during World War II.

In mid-1935, Roosevelt proposed a tax bill that increased inheritance and gift taxes and the progressivity of personal income taxes on higher-income taxpayers. This was the so-called soak-the-rich tax bill. It also proposed a graduated scale of corporate income taxes. All of these were designed to reduce the concentration of wealth. The tax increases would have tended to decrease spending and slow the recovery. Congress provided some offsetting stimulus when in 1935 it passed a bill to provide additional early payments of World War I veterans' bonuses. Roosevelt promptly vetoed the bill. Similar to what had happened to Hoover's 1931 veto of a comparable bill, Congress overrode Roosevelt's veto. As a result, federal spending increased by $1.4 billion in 1936 because of the early bonus payments. This action tended to provide some stimulus to economic activity. But the Treasury had to borrow funds in the capital markets in order to make these payments, and this reduction of funds available for private investment reduced economic activity and probably offset any stimulus provided by the bonus money.

Another measure—the Wheeler-Rayburn bill—was intended as a death sentence for public utility holding companies because of its requirement that, unless the companies could prove that they were essential to the generation and distribution of electricity, they be dissolved in five years. The final bill moved less aggressively on this point but did provide greater federal control over the financial activities of public utilities and greater regulatory control over utility rates. The Banking Act of 1935 also caused a furor. It reorganized the Federal Reserve System to give clear control to the Board of Governors in Washington, D.C., and reduced federal government influence by removing the comptroller of the currency and the secretary of treasury from the governing board. But economists, bankers, and the American Banking Association were outraged by Title II of the proposed bill. This section gave the president the right to name and remove the chairman and vice chairman of the Board of Governors—and was perceived as a clear attempt to put the Federal Reserve System directly under the president's control. The public outcry was so intense that the section was dropped from the final bill.

The Frankfurter-Brandeis ideal of reducing the power of big business in order to promote small independent businesses was also seen in two bills regulating retail trade. The Miller-Tydings Act, or the fair trade act, exempted resale price-maintenance contracts from the anti-trust laws. This allowed manufacturers to require that retailers charge retail prices set by the manufacturers. It was expected that this would reduce price-cutting and allow small retailers to compete with larger retailers and chain stores. The Robinson-Patman Act, or antichain-store act, stipulated that manufacturers could not price discriminate in favor of larger buyers. In this way it intended to save thousands of small, independent retailers from succumbing to the competition of large chain stores with their massive buying power.

The 1936 tax on undistributed corporate profits was another important initiative of the anti-trusters. They believed that by retaining some corporate profits and using these to finance internal investments, corporate managers were made less directly answerable to stockholders and were freed from competing for funds from external lenders, thus furthering the concentration of wealth and power. By forcing firms to disburse all undistributed corporate profits and stopping firms from retaining profits in the future, the wealthy (who owned most of the corporate stock) would have to pay relatively large income taxes on the additional income and all firms would then have to enter the capital markets to obtain expansion funds. This leveling of the playing field would reduce the disadvantages that smaller firms faced. The measure, as finally passed, was bitterly opposed and criticized by nearly all business groups and by most Republicans.

Finally, the anti-trusters argued that the anti-trust laws needed to be revived and applied after their suppression during the NRA. In 1937 Robert Jackson, the new head of the anti-trust division, initiated several major cases. These included the Madison Oil cases, to address complaints of independent jobbers that major oil companies conspired to rig oil prices; the Alcoa case, charging Alcoa with monopolizing aluminum ingot production; the case charging the automobile manufacturers' financing arms with monopolizing automobile financing; and the Ethyl gasoline case, charging the Ethyl Corporation with a misuse of patents to stabilize gasoline prices. In 1938, when Jackson was appointed solicitor general, Thurman Arnold's appointment to head the anti-trust division was something of a surprise: Arnold had written a biting satire on government anti-trust policy, suggesting there was little chance of ever breaking up large business organizations. But upon his appointment he insisted that, given sufficient money and manpower, the anti-trust division could begin breaking up large businesses and restoring competition in the economy. Arnold inherited the cases that Jackson had started and initiated a number of new cases in order to make the anti-trust laws more effective.

BUILDING AN EXPANDED WELFARE STATE

The counterpart to the attack on big business was the building of an expanded welfare state. The centerpiece of this effort was the Social Security Act of 1935. The bill had three parts. One section established unemployment insurance funded by the federal government but administered by the states. It was to be financed by a tax levied on employers. A second part established old-age insurance (what is now called Social Security) so that the elderly would have some income when they stopped working because of retirement or disability. This was funded by a compulsory tax levied equally on employer and employee. The third part of the act aimed to provide funds for the aged, the crippled and blind, and dependent mothers and their children. The federal government would allocate matching funds to the states for these welfare expenditures.

The Social Security tax had an unintended side effect: as the tax was phased in between 1936 and 1938, it tended to reduce consumers' and businesses' purchasing power, and thus economic activity. But because no one was eligible to begin collecting Social Security payments, there was no offsetting increase in purchasing power. The resulting decrease in net spending was a force working to contract economic activity.

THE WAGNER ACT AND THE RISE OF LABOR UNIONS

As early as 1934, Senator Robert Wagner had concluded that section 7a of the NRA was not working and had written a new act to strengthen labor unions by creating a National Labor Relations Board with enforcement judicial powers. Roosevelt did not support it in 1934, but the next year he did. The Wagner Act, which is often called labor's "Magna Carta," was passed in the summer of 1935. Several other bills also proposed to aid labor. In 1936 the Walsh-Healey Act required firms doing business with the federal government to observe the old NRA wage and labor provisions. The 1938 Fair Labor Standards Act abolished child labor, mandated a minimum wage in covered industries, and called for the payment of overtime wages for work in excess of forty hours a week. It included provisions to adjust the minimum wage over time.

Despite the passage of the Wagner Act, the AFL continued to be reluctant to recruit workers in unorganized industries for fear that multitudes of less-skilled workers would overwhelm the organization. They were also unsure how to organize workers who did not fit into existing skill classifications. In November 1935, John L. Lewis led several unions that were more industrial in structure (that is, they included all the workers in an industry, whatever their skills) to form a Committee for Industrial Organization to begin taking advantage of the new labor law. The AFL strenuously opposed this move because it was forbidden "dual unionism" (creating an organization that could rival the authority of the AFL), and in November 1937 it expelled the unions in the CIO. The CIO unions then formed the rival Congress of Industrial Organizations. Meanwhile, in late 1936 the CIO finally moved to begin organizing under the Wagner Act. Financed largely by the United Mine Workers (UMW), the Amalgamated Clothing Workers Union (ACWU), and the International Ladies' Garment Workers Union (ILGWU), the CIO began organizing drives in a number of industries. In 1937, after the use of sit-down strikes, the CIO organized all the automobile producers except Ford, which successfully fought unionization until 1941. In the steel industry, United States Steel and most small steel producers were organized, but "Little Steel"—the six next-largest firms of Bethlehem, Republic, Youngstown Sheet and Tube, Inland, National, and ARMCO—refused to sign. Ford and Little Steel managed to stave off unionization by granting the same hours and wages as the unionized firms and by using a combination of propaganda, public relations, and force. Successful organizing drives in 1937 also occurred among dockworkers, rubber firms, electrical manufacturers, agricultural implement manufacturers, construction equipment manufacturers, textile firms, and sawmills.

CONTINUED PLANNING

Most of the surviving planners who had been involved with the NRA moved into the Department of Agriculture and scaled back their agenda. They continued to believe in centralized, nationwide planning but no longer had much say in industrial policy. They were limited to agriculture and piecemeal legislation in a few selected industries. After the adverse Supreme Court decision, the Agricultural Adjustment Act was replaced by the Soil Conservation and Domestic Allotment Act. Although ostensibly aimed at conserving soil and other natural resources, it was essentially the AAA without the processing tax. In early 1938 the Soil Conservation Act was updated into the second Agricultural Adjustment Act.

The second AAA included Agriculture Secretary Henry Wallace's concept of an "ever-normal granary" to smooth out the year-to-year carryover of agricultural surpluses through flexible price supports.

The Guffey-Snyder Act of August 1935 brought planning to the bituminous coal industry, but early the next year the Supreme Court invalidated it. The Guffey-Vinson act, passed in early 1937, replaced it and installed price floors, marketing agreements, and coal classifications. When NRA control over the crude oil industry ended, the Federal Bureau of Mines began to provide a regular flow of information on prices and production of crude oil to state agencies. These agencies then began to allocate crude oil production within the industry to control overall production. The planners were also able to make inroads into transportation by placing interstate pipelines, interstate trucking, and interstate airline travel under federal regulation and control.

The ELECTION OF 1936 AND THE ATTACK ON THE SUPREME COURT

The presidential campaign of 1936 almost became class warfare. Roosevelt's acceptance speech for the nomination of his party, written by Thomas Corcoran, was widely regarded as essentially a formal declaration of war against the free enterprise system. Roosevelt charged that "economic royalists" were attempting to regain the power they had held until the depression and at every step were now blocking the needed reforms he proposed.

The strategy behind the president's campaign was to gain the support of progressives and former socialists, workers, farmers, and blacks where they could vote. Thus his tactics included attacks on big business, organized money, the forces of selfishness, and the desire for power. Roosevelt's campaign tended to be divisive and to inspire fear. The Democratic candidates for president in 1924 and 1928, John W. Davis and Al Smith, both deserted Roosevelt and supported the Republican candidate, the Kansan Alf Landon, because of the thrust of FDR's campaign. Roosevelt's first director of the budget, Lewis Douglas, also came out in support of Landon.

The president took further steps to improve his reelection chances. Because the WPA was running short of funds, he directed that additional funding be made available so that thousands of people were not thrown off WPA payrolls on October 1, 1936. He directed Secretary of Agriculture Wallace to do whatever was necessary to ensure that cotton prices did not fall below twelve cents per pound. Soil Conservation checks were sent to farmers shortly before election day.

Alf Landon was the weak candidate of a disorganized Republican party. Roosevelt's divisive campaign effectively brought out many voters. The result was a huge victory for Roosevelt in the 1936 election. In his 1937 State of the Union address, the president hinted at a resurrection of the NRA. Shortly after that he unveiled his plan to "pack" the Supreme Court by appointing an additional justice for each justice who was seventy years old and had served for at least ten years but did not choose to retire. The proposal was clearly designed to allow Roosevelt to load the Court with appointees favorable to his legislation, and was widely denounced. In June the Senate Judiciary Committee reported out the bill with a recommendation so negative that no attempt was made to resurrect it. The battle over Roosevelt's court-packing bill consumed an entire congressional session and split the Democratic party. It cost the president some of his support and helped destroy his aura of invincibility.

THE 1937–1938 DEPRESSION

By early 1937 naysayers were pointing to a few nagging worries. Current prices were showing signs of faster increase by late 1936 and early 1937. Both Leon Henderson, who had moved from the NRA to the Securities and Exchange Commission, and Federal Reserve Board Chairman Marriner Eccles sent memos to Roosevelt expressing their concerns that monopolistic firms were excessively raising prices and wages. Henderson thought that, if not checked, the price increases could bring on a recession by the end of the year. In April 1937, Roosevelt agreed that some prices were unjustifiably high. He singled out several industries and implied that monopolistic practices lay behind some of the price increases. Wage rates had also begun to rise at a more rapid rate. A number of firms had surprised the administration by using some of their undistributed corporate profits to pay bonuses and raise wage rates for employees as well as to pay additional dividends to stockholders instead of paying as much in the new undistributed corporate profits taxes. An explosion of labor strife in 1937 brought strikes for union recognition as well as higher wages, shorter hours, and other benefits.

By mid-1937 the economy had stopped expanding. The *New York Herald-Tribune* index of business activity began declining in early 1937, and by April its index showed that all of 1936's gains had disappeared. The Federal Reserve Board's index of industrial production showed that economic activity peaked in May 1937 and declined slowly through September. Most profit reports for the second quarter showed disappointing results and were expected to be worse in the third quarter. The Standard and Poor's index of industrial stock prices began falling after March 1937 and was down 20 percent by September. On October 18 the stock market crashed almost as severely as in 1929. Between August 1937 and April 1938 the Standard and Poor's index fell nearly 52 percent. For comparison, over the period of September 1929 to May 1930 the index fell about 25 percent.

As the depression gathered momentum, industrial production plummeted. From September 1937 to June 1938 durable manufacturing production fell more than 66 percent while nondurable manufacturing production fell almost 15 percent. Over the course of the entire contraction from May 1937 to May 1938, durable manufacturing production declined 67 percent. This extraordinarily rapid contraction was more severe than over comparable periods in the 1920–1921 depression or the 1929–1930 phase of the Great Depression. The stock market collapse between August and December 1937 matched the severity of the production decline; stock prices fell 41.5 percent between August and December, and fell another 10 percent by the time they reached bottom in April 1938. The unemployment rate rose from 12.3 percent in May 1937 to 20.1 percent in May 1938. Another estimate found that the number of unemployed workers rose from 5.1 million in August and September 1937 to 10.8 million in May 1938. Prices also stopped rising. The Consumer Price Index declined by 1.9 percent between 1937 and 1938 and by another 1.4 percent between 1938 and 1939, even though the economy began to recover after May 1938. Wholesale prices fell almost 9.5 percent between 1937 and 1938. Although wholesale prices had fallen at the same rate between 1929 and 1930, consumer prices now fell at a slower rate than before.

The contraction cast a pall over the entire Roosevelt program. In the spring of 1937 many observers had argued that a contraction was remote because the economy was still so far from full employment. Most did not expect a depression within a depression, and certainly no one expected the ferocious decline that occurred. But the new depression brought the economy back to where it had been in 1934 and shook everyone's confidence in the economy and the New Deal.

WHAT CAUSED THE DEPRESSION WITHIN A DEPRESSION?

Roosevelt and his advisers already knew whom to blame for the depression of 1937–1938. Leon Henderson and Marriner Eccles had suggested that excessive price increases by monopolies could bring on a recession, and they now believed that events had justified their concerns. In 1938, Roosevelt charged that monopolies had brought on the new depression and called for a commission to study the growth and nature of monopoly power in the United States. The Temporary National Economic Commission was established and began commissioning various studies of monopolies and their power. The full set of studies did not appear until 1941, when other events overshadowed the concern about the growth of monopoly power.

But the new depression was not brought on by monopoly businesses arbitrarily increasing prices. There were, in fact, two different primary sources that were jointly responsible for this contraction: the actions of the Federal Reserve System, and the rapid rise in wage rates and labor costs during the great unionization drives in early 1937.

In mid-1929 the nation's banks had held $7.50 in reserves for each $100 in deposits. By July 1936 they held $18.48 in reserves for each $100 in deposits. Bank reserves were almost double what the law required. In addition, banks had invested a much larger portion of their deposits in very safe but extremely low-yield short-term securities. Three-month government bills had a rate of return of .14 percent in 1935, ninety-day stock exchange loans an interest rate of .55 percent, long-term U.S. bonds a yield of 2.79 percent, high-grade municipal bonds a yield of 3.40 percent, and short-term bank loans to businesses in large cities an average interest rate of 2.90 percent. Bank investments in securities had risen from 23.9 percent of liabilities in 1929 to 40.3 percent of liabilities in 1935.

Federal Reserve officials were concerned by the large build-up of banks' excess reserves following the end of the contraction. They reasoned that the accumulation of excess reserves was chiefly due to a lack of demand for business loans, as evidenced by low interest rates and a rise in bank investments as compared with bank loans. If business loan demand recovered, the Fed reasoned, the large excess reserves would allow banks quickly to increase their lending and, in the process, the money supply would also quickly expand. A rapid expansion of the money supply would result in inflation. And Federal Reserve officials were not about to allow price inflation in the American economy.

The Banking Act of 1935 had given the Federal Reserve System new authority to double reserve requirements. After studies that showed the excess reserves were widely distributed geographically and across all sizes of member banks, the Federal Reserve began to raise reserve requirements. They were confident that this would do nothing except eliminate excess reserves and thereby remove a potential source of future inflation. Between August 16, 1936, and May 1, 1937, in three steps, the reserve requirements for central reserve city banks in New York City and Chicago were doubled, from 13 percent to 26 percent; the reserve requirement for reserve city banks was doubled, from 10 to 20 percent; and the reserve requirement for country banks was doubled, from 7 to 14 percent. The largest part of these increases occurred on August 16.

If Federal Reserve officials had been correct, the only noticeable effect should have been a decrease in banks' excess reserves. Excess reserves did initially decline, but, contrary to Fed expectations, by mid-1937 they began to rise again, and by mid-1938 excess reserves had generally been restored to levels that preceded the increases in reserve requirements. If banks wanted the excess reserves, perhaps as a buffer against unexpected depositor demands, banks would try to restore the excess reserves that the Fed had so carefully wiped out. To do so they would have held fewer bonds and short-term securities, and reduced lending. Reduced demand for bonds would cause bond prices to fall—and, indeed, bond prices began falling by the end of 1936 and fell into the second quarter of 1937. Interest rates on treasury bills began rising by the fall of 1936 and continued to rise into the second quarter of 1937, and prime commercial paper rates rose sharply on March 1, 1937. From December 1936 to December 1937, the money supply fell 5.7 percent. The powerful contractionary policy initiated by the Fed with its increase in reserve requirements reduced the money supply and helped bring on the 1937–1938 depression.

The second major source of the new depression was a sharp rise in labor costs from the end of 1936 through the first half of 1937. This was the result of the new Social Security taxes that employers had to pay, the new tax on undistributed corporate profits, and the rise in unionization. The new Social Security taxes began to be collected in 1936 and 1937. For firms with employees subject to this tax, labor costs increased because of the employer's share of the tax. At the end of 1936, many firms reacted to the new undistributed corporate profits tax by paying bonuses, raising wage rates, and increasing dividends. The excess profits tax also led businesses to begin reducing their investment spending, and this independently helped bring on the depression. For twenty-five manufacturing industries for which data is available, average money wage rates had risen very slowly, from 60 cents per hour in June 1935 to 61.9 cents per hour in October 1936. In November 1936 this average wage rate rose to 62.4 cents and then to 63.9 cents in December 1936—an annual rate of increase of 19 percent over those two months—and fell slightly in January 1937.

The second factor in the wage rate increases were the unionization drives of 1937. After the successful sit-down strike forced General Motors to recognize the United Automobile Workers (UAW) as a bargaining agent and sign a contract on February 10, 1937, wage rates were immediately raised by five cents an hour, the workweek was limited to five eight-hour days, and work in excess of forty hours a week was to be paid time and a half. The automobile manufacturers Hudson, Packard, and Studebaker, and the component suppliers Briggs Body, Murray Body, Motor Products, Timken–Detroit Axle, and many others quickly followed with contracts very similar to GM's. On April 6, Chrysler signed on terms identical to GM. Ford refused to recognize the UAW but raised its wage rate to the GM level as well as adopting the forty-hour workweek and overtime pay rate.

In the steel industry the key was United States Steel, the industry's largest firm. U.S. Steel employed 50 percent more workers than the next three largest steel firms combined. The steel industry had enjoyed a significant recovery after mid-1935 and appeared to be ready for organizing drives. In 1936 the Steel Workers' Organizing Committee, SWOC, began contacting employees at U.S. Steel. As its members took over offices in the company unions, these unions at U.S. Steel and other steel firms became more and more independent and adversarial. Responding in November 1936, firms in the steel industry increased their wage rates from 47 cents an hour to 52.5 cents an hour (an increase of 11.7 percent). In January and February, John L. Lewis and Myron Taylor of U.S. Steel entered into negotiations and on March 2, U.S. Steel recognized the union that became the United Steel Workers (USW). Wage rates were increased to 62.5 cents an hour—a 19 percent increase—the workweek was set at eight hours a day for a five-day week, and time and a half was to be paid for overtime work. By May 1, similar contracts had been signed with 110 other smaller steel firms. The next six largest steel firms, "Little Steel" (Bethlehem, Republic, Youngstown Sheet and Tube, Inland, National, and American Rolling Mill), refused to bargain with the SWOC but raised their wage rates to U.S. Steel levels and offered the same hour and overtime provisions. Between October 1936 and May 1937 wage rates in the steel industry had increased from 47 cents to 62.5 cents an hour—an increase of 33 percent from the October wage rate.

Other large industries also were unionized in 1937. John Deere, International Harvester, Caterpillar, and other firms in the agricultural and construction machinery industry recognized the UAW. Goodyear, Goodrich, and other rubber firms were organized in April 1937, and Westinghouse, General Electric, and other electrical manufacturers somewhat later. In all these industries, wage rates immediately increased with the signing of a union contract.

The result was an upward surge in wage rates in durable manufacturing industries in the first part of 1937. Average wage rates for 25 manufacturing industries increased from 63.8 cents in January 1937 to 71.1 cents in July 1937—an increase of 11.4 percent from the January base. By July 1937 this average wage rate had risen 14.9 percent from the October 1936 rate of 61.9 cents an hour. The increase in the wage rate understates the increase in labor costs because the restriction of the workweek to five eight-hour days with time and a half for overtime, and the initial implementation of union work rules, further increased labor costs. Wages in these durable manufacturing industries increased sharply with no increases in demand for what the firms produced and no increases in labor productivity. Firms faced a dilemma: if they raised prices, sales would fall, and production and employment would decline; if they did not raise prices, their profits would decline. Most firms began reducing employment and production.

At the same time labor cost increases were hitting these manufacturing firms, the Federal Reserve's restrictive monetary policy began to take effect. As banks began to restore excess reserves, lending fell, interest rates rose, and aggregate demand began to fall—especially for the durable business and consumer goods these manufacturing firms produced. With falling demand, it was no longer an issue of raising prices—in some cases prices were reduced as production and employment began to fall. By the fall of 1937 the profits of manufacturing firms had fallen sharply and were expected to fall even further—and the stock market crashed. The result was the severe but relatively short depression between May 1937 and May 1938.

RECOVERY FROM THE 1937–1938 DEPRESSION

As a result of extensive criticism of the tax on undistributed corporate profits, and the suggestion that it helped bring on the depression, Congress in April 1938 reduced it to inconsequential rates. Roosevelt did not favor this retreat on taxation but could not veto it successfully and it became law without his signature.

Through 1938, Roosevelt continued to resist calls to moderate his programs and provide more freedom for business. He now had almost no support in the business community, was rapidly losing what support he had in the press, and was being deserted by Democrats in the Senate and House. A government reorganization bill he sent to Congress was overwhelmingly defeated, with more than half the negative votes cast by Democrats. In the 1938 elections the Republicans gained eighty-one seats in the House and eight seats in the Senate, and most political pundits viewed the election as a defeat for Roosevelt and the New Deal. After the Munich crisis in September 1938, many historians argue that Roosevelt reached an implicit understanding with Southern Democrats. In return for their support of his foreign and defense policies, he would not push new reform initiatives.

In December 1938, to Harry Hopkins's surprise, Roosevelt nominated Hopkins as secretary of commerce. It was considered a strange appointment because Hopkins had no business experience and was considered an anti-business New Dealer. Surprisingly, however, Hopkins set out to repair relations between the administration and the business community. Hopkins publicly urged changes that would shift the administration's approach from reform to recovery. Many thought Hopkins's pronouncements close to an admission that the Roosevelt administration had been wrong in pushing so hard for reform and had not thought enough about recovery. Secretary of Agriculture Wallace approvingly concurred with Hopkins on the need to emphasize recovery. Treasury Secretary Morgenthau also began making public statements on the need to revitalize business and promote recovery. He suggested that tax legislation not be a deterrent to business activity. This mild palace revolt against the entrenched New Deal reformers—by former New Deal allies no less—apparently began to have its effects. The new battleground became a tax bill that, among other things, imposed a flat 18 percent corporate profits tax and recommended that the undistributed corporate profits tax be allowed to expire. Both the House and the Senate passed the bill over Roosevelt's objections. Hopkins now began moving into the position of key adviser to the president, and gradually the emphasis shifted to recovery and preparedness for a war many thought was ahead. After 1938 no new laws were proposed and no new reform initiatives undertaken.

This retreat was accompanied by a steady, if slow, recovery

from the depression within a depression. In May 1937 the index of durable manufacturing production had reached 94.16 percent of the July 1929 level. After falling to 46.96 percent in June 1938, it remained around 66 to 68 percent of the July 1929 level from November 1938 through May 1939. The last five months of 1939 saw a more rapid increase in production, the index again moving to 96 percent of the July 1929 peak. Employment did not recover as rapidly. Through the summer of 1938 the unemployment rate hovered around 20 percent. It dropped below 17 percent in the fall of 1938 and then increased to better than 19 percent for most of the winter and spring of 1939. Spurred by the foreign demand for war materials, durable manufacturing expanded in the fall of 1939 while the unemployment rate declined to about 14 percent.

Although unemployment fell, factory employment in twenty-five manufacturing industries in March 1940 remained at only 90 percent of the employment level reached in May 1937. And the average wage rate in those industries saw no change until late 1939. That manufacturing production recovered faster than manufacturing employment was not surprising. The unionization surge in 1937 had sharply raised labor costs relative to capital and resource costs. As the recovery occurred, firms began to produce using somewhat more capital and somewhat less labor in response to the changes in relative costs.

By the beginning of 1940 the American economy was roughly back where it had been in mid-1937—and still a long way from full employment. The recovery after the 1937–1938 depression was slow, just as the recovery after the end of the NRA was slow. In nearly two years of recovery between July 1935 and May 1937, the unemployment rate had declined from 21.3 to 12.3 percent, but the unemployment rate in May 1937 was still far above full-employment levels with considerable idleness of buildings and machinery. The unemployment rate in the summer of 1939 was similar to the unemployment rate in the early summer of 1938. By early 1940 the economy had revived only to May 1937 levels. Why, when the recovery did begin, first in 1935–1937 and then in 1938–1940, was it so slow?

Some of the slow decline in unemployment may have been due to work relief programs. All individuals employed at government work relief programs (the PWA, Public Works Administration; WPA, Works Progress Administration; CCC, Civilian Conservation Corps; and the like) were counted as unemployed. There is evidence that by the late 1930s some workers had begun to consider these as equivalent to full-time jobs. A 1940 census sample found that a large percentage of WPA workers had been employed by work relief programs for quite long periods of time, at least since the previous year. Although wage rates were somewhat lower, work was steady and predictable, and apparently some workers were reluctant to leave work relief for the more risky private sector.

But the root of the lag in economic recovery lay in private investment, the most important component of overall spending. It allows the economy to grow and is important in determining the overall level of income. During the depression, by far the worst unemployment had been found in the industrial areas of the Midwest and East. Durable manufacturing production, which is primarily the production of investment goods, declined much more dramatically than the production of nondurable goods and services. Construction of houses, apartments, retail and office buildings, and manufacturing plants virtually ceased. The key to restoring the economy lay in restoring private investment. But this did not happen. From 1931 through 1935 private investment was insufficient to replace the capital stock that was wearing out—in other words, *net* investment was a negative $18 billion in those years. Over the entire decade from 1930 to 1940, private in-

vestment was so low that net private investment was a negative $3 billion. Private investment began to recover in 1941
and then was shut down by the war economy. Finally in 1946,
for the first time since 1929, private net investment boomed
and the United States returned to full employment.

There are several explanations for the slow recovery of private investment during the 1930s. Business investment in
structures and machinery and equipment faced structural impediments. The largest industries tended to be mature and
slow growing, or even declining, making it difficult for them
to generate the investment demand necessary to reemploy
workers. Expanding sectors, such as consumer nondurable
goods and services and durable consumer goods (such as lux-
ury automobiles, appliances, and communications) could not
generate enough investment to compensate for declines in sectors such as primary metals, textiles, and lumber, which were
much larger employers.

Residential construction, a major source of investment, suffered from its own problems. In the speculative boom in residential construction in the twenties, residential construction
had exceeded 8 percent of GNP. The collapse of residential
construction after 1929 was just as striking as the previous
boom. Not until 1951 did residential construction reach the
level achieved in 1929.

The rise of the automobile led to speculative housing developments around most large cities. Developers, anticipating the
growth of suburban housing, quickly obtained land that could
be developed as housing sites and then began the infrastructure development of streets, electric lines, and other utilities in
hopes of attracting buyers. Poorly planned, uncoordinated,
and excessive development led to a decline in residential construction between 1927 and 1929. With the collapse of housing
development after 1929, many unfinished developments were
simply abandoned. The most notorious examples of halted

projects could be found in south Florida, but they occurred in many other areas. In 1934, 59 percent of the lots in Westchester County (a suburb of New York City) were undeveloped, and in suburban Buffalo, 81 percent of the lots were undeveloped. In 1938, 95 percent of the lots in four townships surrounding Detroit were undeveloped.

In many cases owners simply walked away from their projects. Many had been pledged as collateral elsewhere, producing great uncertainty about ownership of lots. A recovery of residential construction in the thirties required that these lots be redeveloped, but this proved to be a monumental task. Developers wanted clean land for residential projects. Thus developments where some platting and infrastructure had been accomplished had to be reassembled to begin the investment anew. Finding the owners to purchase and assemble the developments proved to be a formidable task. Discovering the mortgages, liens, and collateral pledges on each lot was just as difficult. And the task of overcoming the legal and physical debris of past subdivisions often proved to be prohibitively expensive. As a result, residential construction remained much more depressed throughout the thirties than other types of investment.

Although these factors slowed the recovery of investment after the contraction ended in 1933, the primary explanation for the slow recovery of private investment in the thirties can be found in the concept of "regime uncertainty." Especially from 1935 on, the New Deal ravaged the confidence of businessmen. As they became less and less certain that private property rights in their capital and its income stream would be protected and maintained—in other words, uncertain about the continuation of the current "regime" of private property rights—they became less and less willing to make investments, especially longer-term investments in structures and long-lived machinery. Increasingly, only short-term investments with quick payoffs were viewed as desirable. Threats to private property rights may come from many sources, including tax increases, new taxes, confiscation of private property, and business regulation that reduces an owner's rights over property.

Government defines these private property rights and maintains and defends them. Without private property rights, market economies cannot function because every transaction is really an exchange of private property rights. If the government threatens or weakens private property rights, it discourages market activity, especially private investment.

In retrospect we know that the United States did not become some sort of socialist state in the 1930s, but this was not so obvious to many businessmen at the time. Many of the administration's actions suggested that such a development might very well occur. New Deal planners made it quite clear that they preferred a planned economy in which government direction would replace business planning. Rexford Tugwell, for one, did not hide his strong leanings in this direction. The New Deal anti-trusters hoped to break up all larger businesses and return to an idyllic world of numerous small businesses where none would have a significant impact on their market.

The list of congressional acts that weakened or threatened to weaken private property rights between 1933 and 1940 is lengthy. Farmers found that in return for higher prices through government programs, their independence in deciding what and how much to produce was significantly constrained. In some cases farmers who had not agreed to participate in a program were assigned quotas and taxed heavily if they produced in excess of their assigned quota. Processors found themselves taxed to provide revenue to help prop up farm incomes.

The NRA's goal was to cartelize American industry and reduce the ability of independent firms to decide on prices, production, and investment. The NRA and then the Wagner Act circumscribed businesses' ability to choose whom to employ and how much to pay. The Securities Acts of 1933 and 1935 made it more difficult for both small and large firms to sell securities in order to reduce (or eliminate) the easier access of larger firms to the capital markets. After 1933 this issue was repeatedly raised by businesses as one of the most important impediments they faced. Banks were forced to separate commercial from investment banking. The right to own gold for monetary purposes was prohibited, and gold clauses in contracts were outlawed. Farm mortgage holders found, during farm mortgage moratoriums, that their legal rights to foreclose on delinquent borrowers had been severely limited.

In the coal and crude oil industries, anti-trust laws were suspended (even after the NRA) so that governments could impose quotas on producers to control the markets. The Tennessee Valley Authority inserted the federal government into the generation of electricity in competition with private utilities. And utilities were told that the TVA would become the yardstick by which private utilities would be measured and regulated. Regulation of interstate trucking, interstate busing, and oil pipelines all appeared in the 1930s, and the regulation of radio and airlines was tightened. Federal laws aimed at preserving small business—the Robinson-Patman Act and the Miller-Tydings Act—limited the rights of larger firms. Tax increases in 1935, 1936, and 1937 were intended to "soak the rich," and numerous new taxes on businesses were imposed. The Fair Labor Standards Act mandated minimum wage rates and the standard forty-hour week with time and a half for overtime work.

After the NRA was declared unconstitutional, the federal government did an about-face and began using the anti-trust laws to prosecute firms for the kind of behavior it had previously encouraged. In 1938 and 1939, Thurman Arnold's prosecution of anti-trust cases and his attack on business concentration and trade practices expanded sharply. Roosevelt proposed packing the Supreme Court to be certain that his laws were upheld. He had proposed being given the authority to name and remove the chairman and vice chairman of the Board of Governors of the Federal Reserve System in order to achieve better control over its policies. And, in 1935, 1936, and 1937 his speeches continued to lash out in a divisive manner at the "royalists" and "dictators" in industry and finance who opposed his programs. Roosevelt condemned "monopolies" for causing the 1937–1938 contraction. In response he initiated the Temporary National Economic Committee (TNEC), which called more than 550 witnesses to determine how monopolies had brought on the recession and ultimately published 43 volumes on monopoly in American industry and how to solve this problem.

Public opinion surveys of businesses at the end of the 1930s provide evidence of this regime uncertainty. Business perceived the Roosevelt administration as anti-business and expected government control of business to accelerate. Polls showed that the overwhelming majority of business leaders believed that a sharp reduction in business confidence had retarded the recovery. As late as 1940 most business leaders did not believe that conditions yet justified planning to expand their operations.

Ordinarily, regime uncertainty reduces the desire of firms for longer-term investments and, especially, the willingness of investors to finance them. Premiums appear in the yields on longer-term bonds. At the end of 1920s there were essentially no premiums on longer-term bonds. From 1931 through 1934, yields increased slightly. For example, the yield on a 30-year bond was 1.6 times the yield on a 1-year bond in 1933. Between 1935 and 1941 these differences increased substantially. For example, in 1936 the yield on 30-year bonds was 5.25

times the yield on 1-year bonds, and the yield on 10-year bonds was 4.33 times the yield on 1-year bonds.

As the NRA collapsed and Roosevelt began his attack on wealth, these differences increased and remained high through 1941, but then fell sharply in 1942 and remained lower throughout World War II. With the onset of the war, Roosevelt realized he needed big business to produce the weapons of war and pulled business leaders into the administration as "dollar-a-day" consultants to organize the war effort, regime uncertainty diminished considerably and premiums on the yields of longer-term bonds fell.

The recovery from mid-1935 to mid-1937 and again after the end of the 1937–1938 depression within a depression was slow because business was reluctant to invest, expand, and undertake potentially risky innovations. They were increasingly uncertain of the rules they were operating under and how secure their property rights were. In the 1930s the Roosevelt administration abruptly and dramatically altered the institutional framework within which private business decisions were made—not just once but several times. The effect was to retard the recovery from the Great Depression of 1929–1933.

5

The Legacy of the Great Depression

THE GREAT DEPRESSION was a landmark in twentieth-century history. In market-oriented economies it provoked a growing intellectual fascination with socialist economic ideas, as exemplified by the Soviet Union. It precipitated World War II, which in turn led to the spread of communism across large reaches of the globe. In the United States, the federal government assumed a new importance in the 1930s—an importance it continues to maintain. It undertook new roles in relief, welfare, regulation, and subsidization, leading to the emergence of the new regulatory state. The unmistakable imprint of the New Deal is seen on the social legislation of the Kennedy-Johnson years and in the growing importance of Washington, D.C., in the eyes of the typical American. Doubts arose in the minds of many people about the virtues of "unfettered market economies." In many ways the Great Depression was the defining moment for twentieth-century America.

The Great Depression, and the slow recovery that followed during the 1930s, was a frustrating experience for everyone. At the time it seemed that no one could offer an acceptable explanation for these events. Conventional economic theory did not seem capable of explaining why the depression had occurred or why it was so long and severe. Neither did there appear to be an adequate explanation for the slow recovery and the 1937–1938 depression. But the experience led an English economist to propose a new theory to explain the depression and how to get out of it. The apparent recovery of the economy with the onset of World War II seemed to validate this new theory and in the postwar era Keynesian macroeconomics, as it came to be called, became a major part of mainstream economic analysis.

WORLD WAR II AND THE RISE OF KEYNESIAN ECONOMICS

In 1936, John Maynard Keynes published a new theory intended to explain why economic fluctuations occurred and how stability and full employment in a depressed economy could be restored. Keynes's new theory was a departure from the economic theory of the time. Before 1936 the dominant economic theory was one of markets. It described how the system of relative (or real) prices allocated resources among the different markets so that, in the aggregate, the employment of resources resulted in the production of those commodities and services on which individuals placed the greatest values. Its basis was in the utility-maximizing behavior of individual consumers and the profit-maximizing behavior of individual producers. The primary coordinating mechanisms were flexible relative (or real) prices.

Keynes took a different approach. Rather than considering individual markets, such as the market for shoes, the market for loaves of bread, the market for haircuts, and so forth, he examined aggregate sectors of the economy—specifically the household sector, the business sector, the government sector, and the rest-of-the-world. Aggregate consumer spending represented the demands from households for newly produced goods and services. Businesses' demands for newly produced goods and services were represented by aggregate investment spending by all business firms. Aggregate government spending represented the demands of governments for newly produced goods and services. Thus all domestic demands for new goods and services could be classified as consumption, investment, or government spending. Demands for new domestic production from the rest of the world could be represented as net exports (or exports minus imports).

Keynes argued that the key to understanding the performance of the economy was to determine why aggregate demand was sometimes insufficient to employ all the economy's resources. To do that, one had to look at the components of aggregate demand for the economy's new production, or Gross National Product (GNP). Because every dollar of production must be exactly matched by a dollar of income to the owners of the resources that produced the products and services, GNP must be equal to Gross National Income (Y). Keynes argued that consumption spending depended on income; consumption spending alone could not determine the level of income (and therefore economic activity). Investment was determined by the expected profitability of new capital, and this depended primarily on interest rates, expected prices, and other costs of what was produced. Government spending, on the other hand, was determined by social priorities. Because investment did not depend directly on income, it had the power to determine the level of income. If investment spending fell—because, for example, business leaders became more pessimistic about expected profits—production (GNP) and income (Y) would decline.

Keynes argued that a contraction such as the Great Depression was the result of an independent decline in investment spending. To spur the recovery there had to be an independent increase in spending in order to boost aggregate demand. Increased aggregate demand would then automatically begin increasing economic activity, leading to more consumption spending and moving the economy closer to full employment. In severe depressions, Keynes argued, lower interest rates did little to spur additional investment spending. Government, however, was not constrained by income or profits. Thus governments could initiate the necessary increase in aggregate demand to begin increasing GNP. The federal government could do this directly by increasing spending without increasing taxes, or it could to it indirectly by holding government spending constant while decreasing taxes. The decreased taxes would lead to additional disposable income for consumers and businesses and thus to increases in their spending. The tactic of changing government spending and/or taxes was called "fiscal policy." Keynes argued that fiscal policy could be used to increase aggregate demand and move the economy toward full employment when the private sector (consumption and investment spending) did not do so. Before the 1930s the concept of fiscal policy was unknown. Government spending and taxation were designed to produce and distribute those necessary products and services that the private sector did not produce, or did not produce in adequate amounts.

This new theory was initially controversial. Keynes visited the United States after publication of his book, *The General Theory of Employment, Interest and Money.* He met with Roosevelt and urged him adopt an expansionary fiscal policy to end the depression, but the meeting did not go well and neither Keynes nor Roosevelt was impressed with the other. After the 1937–1938 depression there is some evidence that Roosevelt began to accept some additional federal spending as a simple means of increasing total spending. But by 1940 it is safe to say that Keynes's new theory of macroeconomics was still not widely accepted in the discipline of economics and had little impact on public policy.

As the United States began to build its military and naval

forces in 1940 in response to the worsening international situation, on October 29 Roosevelt initiated the first peacetime draft in the nation's history. With Japan's attack on Pearl Harbor on December 7, 1941, the United States moved to a rapid military buildup. Federal government purchases increased from $15 billion in 1940 to $36.2 billion in 1941, an increase of 141.3 percent. They rose to $98.9 billion in 1942, a 173.2 percent increase, and to $147.8 billion in 1943, a 49.4 percent increase. Between 1940 and 1943 real federal expenditures increased 885.3 percent. Tax receipts increased 182.0 percent over the same period. This massive increase in government spending relative to government tax receipts was exactly the type of stimulus that Keynes had proposed.

The unemployment rate fell from 14.6 percent in 1940 to 9.9 percent in 1941, to 4.7 percent in 1942, and to 1.9 percent in 1943. In those years real GNP per person increased 43.3 percent. Using conventional measures, by early 1942, under the impetus of war expenditures, the United States had returned to full employment. Thus it quickly became an article of faith among many economists that increased federal expenditures associated with the war had demonstrated the power of the Keynesian model. There now was a way for the federal government to use its spending and taxing powers to stabilize the economy at, or near to, full employment. Between 1945 and 1965, Keynesian macroeconomics dominated the economic analysis of the overall economy.

MONETARY POLICY DURING THE WAR

The conclusion that Keynesian fiscal policy, applied in the urgent war spending, pushed the economy back to full employment in the early 1940s remained largely intact until the early 1960s. By then, however, economists armed with new estimates of the money supply from the turn of the century through 1960, began to reassess the role of monetary policy as compared with fiscal policy.

In the aftermath of the depressed 1930s, the Federal Reserve System had argued that it had done what it could to reduce the severity of the contraction and speed recovery. Fed officials rationalized that an easy money policy did little good when the economy was so depressed. Later analysis showed that in fact the Federal Reserve, bound by the rules of the gold standard and consumed with worries about inflation, had not engaged in an expansionary, or easy, monetary policy in the 1930s. But as the clouds of war thickened over Europe and the Far East, the Fed had changed its stance and moved to increase the money supply. From December 1939 to December 1940 the money supply grew 15.2 percent; grew another 13.9 percent from 1940 to 1941; 26.2 percent from 1941 to 1942; and 24.4 percent from December 1942 to December 1943. Overall between December 1939 and December 1943 the money supply grew 79.6 percent. This massive increase was engineered by the Federal Reserve System to accommodate the federal government's war demands. Under normal conditions such a huge increase in the money supply would initiate a vigorous expansion in economic activity. In this case, a major aim of expansionary policy was to finance the rapidly increasing federal debt.

The federal government could increasingly spend more than it received in tax revenues because the Fed monetized the growing debt. One way the Fed did this was through the direct purchase of bonds newly issued by the federal government. More important, member banks were allowed to buy short-term government securities and pay for these with deposit credits. The securities were then discounted at the Fed, which, in this process, created additional reserves for the banks to use. The Fed had reached an agreement with the Treasury to peg the price of Treasury bills (mostly ninety-day government securities) to keep their interest rate at three-eighths of 1 percent—an agreement that continued through 1947.

Thus short-term Treasury bills were like interest-bearing cash. To do this the Fed had to discount whatever short-term Treasury bills were offered to it. As a result, bank reserves and the money supply grew sharply. Monetary policy, or more correctly the Fed's agreement with the Treasury to create whatever bank reserves were demanded, therefore played a crucial role in allowing the government's deficit spending—or expansionary fiscal policy. It is unlikely that the federal government's gigantic increase in deficit spending could have occurred without the support of the Federal Reserve System.

THE DECLINE IN UNEMPLOYMENT DURING THE WAR

The reigning view is that the American economy quickly recovered from the depressed 1930s at the beginning of World War II, and that the war years from 1942 through 1945 represented a period of prosperity for American citizens. The foundation for this common view is the dramatic reduction in unemployment, the rise in real consumption spending, and the sharp rise in real GNP during the war years. But close inspection of these foundations reveals that they cannot bear the weight of the "war prosperity" conclusion.

Consider first the sharp decline in unemployment. The number of unemployed in the United States declined from 8.12 million in 1940 to 5.56 million in 1941 to 2.66 million in 1942 to 1.07 million in 1943. Yet at the same time the number of unemployed was falling, the number serving in the military was rising sharply—especially after the October 1940 initiation of the peacetime draft. As the number of unemployed workers fell by 7.05 million between 1940 and 1943, the number in the military services rose by 8.59 million. By 1945 there were 12.12 million in military service, most of whom had been drafted. The huge buildup of military personnel—not the expansion of economic activity—sharply reduced the unemployment rate.

And it is hard to argue that the unemployed men conscripted into military service were better off. Pay was low, with substantial risks of death or serious injury—405,399 died and 670,846 were wounded during the war. The decline in unemployment during the war years is hardly a sign of prosperity in that period.

CONSUMPTION AND INVESTMENT DURING THE WAR

Another cornerstone of the "war prosperity" perception of the early 1940s economy is that the United States produced more of both "guns" (war materials) and "butter" (civilian goods and services). This conclusion too is questionable. During the war years the federal government extensively used price controls and rationing by coupons as its primary means of transferring resources to the government for military production. In the government-directed economy during the war, many civilian firms were ordered to cease civilian production and produce war materials. There were no cars, stoves, refrigerators, and many other types of durable civilian goods produced during the war. The production of many nondurable civilian goods was sharply curtailed. For example, nearly all of the production of automotive-type tools was directed to military use rather than to the civilian economy. Most new tires went to the military and to other priority uses such as over-the-road trucking. To reduce consumer demand for new tires, gasoline was rationed (and price controlled) to reduce driving and thus reduce the demand for tires for civilian automobile use. To ensure a "fair" distribution of what was produced for civilians, ration coupons were distributed allowing civilians to buy, at low controlled prices, their allotment. The rationing was extensive. Had there been no rationing with price controls, excess demand would have driven up prices sharply for the reduced supplies of civilian goods. With rationing and price controls, civilians were unable to spend all of their income on civilian goods and services and were, in essence, forced to save more—and this additional saving was used to buy war bonds to allow the federal government to obtain more resources to produce war materials. The Federal Reserve System's rapid increase of the money supply also allowed the federal government to bid resources away from civilian uses.

During the war the government instituted huge increases in personal and corporate income tax rates as well as many other taxes, such as estate and gift taxes. For individuals, personal exemptions were slashed and rates increased. The top marginal personal income tax rate was raised to 94 percent and applied to all adjusted gross income in excess of $200,000. The application of withholding at the source reduced income tax evasion. Before the war only about the top 30 percent of income earners in the United States had paid personal income taxes. World War II extended the income tax so that virtually every family paid it.

By using taxes, price controls, and rationing, the government thus sought to reduce consumption spending throughout the war. It would indeed be surprising if civilian consumption had increased during the war. Although officially reported statistics show some rise in real consumption spending, the data are suspect. It is well known that official measures significantly understated price inflation in the 1942–1945 period because of extensive price controls and rationing—official prices were kept largely constant, especially after 1943. In some "black market" sales, retailers and consumers sold and resold items at prices in excess of legal price ceilings, but the authorities worked to control such illegal sales. Further, the quality of many goods deteriorated, hiding additional price increases, while other civilian goods simply disappeared due to the government's directives on production. Adjustments to correct for these problems produce figures that show significant declines in consumption during the war. Simultaneously consumers were working longer and harder. Many had to bear the costs of moving long distances to work in war factory centers. Rent controls led to deterioration in housing. With no cars produced, gasoline rationed, and spare parts hard to come by, transportation became more difficult. Price controls and excess demands made searching for commodities longer and harder. Civilians were not better off because of the war.

Investment spending also fell. Although some investment in new plants and equipment occurred where this was necessary to produce war materials, it was insufficient to maintain investment spending. In fact wartime investment was inadequate to offset the depreciation of existing capital. During the war, as during 1930–1933, the capital stock of buildings and equipment in the American economy declined.

With declining consumption and declining private investment, it is difficult to conclude that World War II was a period of "prosperity" for Americans.

What Confidence Do We Have in World War II Economic Data?

The rapid rise in real GNP during the war years is the third piece of evidence for war prosperity brought on by war-induced expansionary Keynesian fiscal policy. But it is widely recognized that the price indices significantly understated inflation during the war years. With price controls in effect, a price index cannot possibly show any inflation that may be occurring—the inflation is hidden. When price controls were largely removed in 1946, price levels quickly rose—not because there suddenly was new inflation but because prices were now able to reflect the hidden inflation that had occurred in previous years. This means that the real production (GNP) of the war years (1942–1945) is overstated.

We also know that the value of federal government production, which dominated the rising real GNP of the war years, is overstated. Some types of war production were overpriced. In the federal government's harried efforts to get the production of war materials under way, it often entered into generous contracts. As munitions production grew dramatically during the war and producers better learned how to produce munitions, productivity rose and costs fell. Thus the real price of munitions fell. But the Commerce Department never acknowledged this in its estimates. When reasonable adjustments are made for the understatement of inflation and the true decline in the price of munitions, real GNP is lower during the war years and rises sharply in 1946 with the release of resources from military production and the ending of price controls and rationing. The Commerce Department has acknowledged that wartime inflation was understated and the real value of munitions production overstated, but it has continually failed to adjust official GNP figures for the war years.

Nor can we truly compare GNP figures during the war years of 1942–1945 with the GNP figures of earlier and later years, given the command economy conditions of the war years. The government controlled prices, rationed goods in an essentially arbitrary manner through coupons and other non-price mechanisms, and directed production in order to achieve maximum effectiveness in producing war materials. This is the opposite of what a free society does. The measured aggregate production (GNP) under a command economy is hardly comparable to a free-market economy's aggregate production.

An example can illustrate this. Suppose a society produces in a year 3 million music CDs, 200,000 cars, 20,000 stoves and 2 million pairs of shoes. If we were to measure production by the number of physical units produced, we could certainly increase aggregate production by reallocating resources away from car and stove production, which require greater resources per car or stove, to the production of music CDs and shoes, which require considerably fewer resources per unit. Suppose that reducing car production by 50,000 cars allows this society to produce an additional 1 million music CDs and an additional 500,000 pairs of shoes. Aggregate production will rise from 5,220,000 units of *things* to 6,670,000 units of *things*.

Would this make the citizens of that society better off? The purpose of production is not to simply produce *things*, no matter what those *things* are. The purpose is to use scarce resources to produce those commodities and services that citizens value more highly. To determine this we weight each unit produced by its price in order to determine the value of production *according to the preferences of the society's citizens*. We then sum up this value of units to obtain the total value of production, or GNP. Consider the effect of this in the original example above. Suppose a music CD has a value (or price) of $15, a car has a value of $20,000, a stove has a value of $1,000, and a pair of shoes has a value of $40. The total value of the production (GNP) then is $4.145 billion. If car production is reduced to increase the production of music CDs and shoes, the total value of the production (GNP) is then $3.18 billion. By this calculation, the citizens of the society are worse off because the economy is producing less of those things on which the citizens place a greater value. In other words, real GNP (GNP with constant prices) has declined.

Why would this society choose to increase the production of music CDs and shoes? In a free-market society this would occur if consumers began placing a greater value on music CDs and shoes and a smaller value on cars and stoves. The change in consumer valuations would be seen in rising prices for music CDs and shoes and falling prices for cars and stoves. Profit-oriented businesses would begin reducing the production of cars and stoves in order to produce more music CDs and shoes. This reallocation of resources (along with further relative price changes) would continue until it was no longer profitable to continue altering production. Prices thus play an absolutely crucial role in allocating resources to production and determining the total value of goods and services.

But this could not happen in the command economy of the years during World War II. Prices were controlled and not allowed to change relative to other prices (except by government directive), or to rise. Prices below market-clearing levels resulted in excess demands for most commodities. To allocate the scarce goods, the government used coupons and other rationing devices. Because prices were controlled, consumers could not show which commodities were more highly valued. The price of, say, a new suit in 1944 cannot be compared to the price of a new suit in 1938 or 1948 because of price controls. In addition, the consumer price index includes the price of purchasing a new car and other durable consumer goods such as a new stove or a new typewriter. How can one create such a price index, or output index, for the years 1942–1945 when cars, stoves, or typewriters (and most other durable consumer goods) were not produced because the government commanded that they not be produced? Price indexes and output indexes for the war years are simply not comparable to the nonwar years.

WHAT DID HAPPEN IN THE 1940S?

In 1940 and 1941 the American economy was beginning to recover from the depressed thirties. The growth of domestic and overseas demand was fueling the expansion of what was, generally, a free-market economy. With the war the United States became a command economy producing what the government demanded—and it demanded war materials. The United States exceeded everyone's expectations in the production of war materials, especially those of its enemies. With its prodigious output, America became the "arsenal of democracy," producing several hundred thousand planes, nearly a hundred thousand tanks, millions of small arms, billions of rounds of small-arms ammunition, thousands of ships, and countless other war materials.

Although the command economy worked well in producing what government wanted, this was not the case with nonwar materials. In fact, authorities attempted to reduce the production of nonwar (or nonessential) commodities and services—and they succeeded. When the command structure began to be dismantled in 1946, price controls were lifted (though not all and not immediately), rationing ended, and war contracts were canceled. Men and women were released from military service. In this suddenly freer environment, consumers finally began to demand more and producers were finally free to expand production and invest more as long as it was profitable for them to do so—and it was profitable. The market economy came back to life and prosperity prevailed. The long depression was finally over.

There are several reasons why so many Americans believed that prosperity reappeared *during* rather than *after* the war. Misleading and inaccurate official government statistics, which are still used today, showed a return to prosperity. As the military draft accelerated, unemployment disappeared and so did the anxiety associated with worries about bringing home a regular paycheck. Patriotic enthusiasm in supporting the war effort buoyed people's spirits, and they were willing to put up with rationing, price controls, and scarcity, though this spirit waned toward the end of the war. People were earning unprecedented amounts of money. Even though they could not spend much of it, they saw their investment in war bonds as increases in their wealth. The war years also saw greater income gains for the poorer members of society, contributing to a general impression of more prosperous conditions. Finally, the war years replaced the pessimistic outlook that so many Americans had developed during the depression and slow recovery of the 1930s with a new optimism, with the expectation that life would be better as the economy turned out enormous quantities of war materials. When the war ended, the optimism of consumers and producers translated into huge increases in demand for consumer products, and the profits of businesses led them to increase production and investment. On the basis of this optimism, stock prices, which had been depressed during the war, were bid up sharply in the postwar years. Prosperity did not return with the war, but the war did set the stage for the return of prosperity beginning in 1946. The election of a more conservative Congress in 1946 led to the rapid end of wage and price controls and the passage of the Taft-Hartley Act, which placed restrictions on labor unions. These measures helped restore business confidence and led to a postwar boom in the United States.

KEYNESIAN ECONOMICS AND POSTWAR FEDERAL GOVERNMENT DEFICITS

Although the economy finally recovered after 1945, the federal government operated differently than it had before the Great Depression. The interaction of the Great Depression and the rise of Keynesian economics led to the acceptance of continuing peacetime budget deficits. Before the 1930s, peacetime federal budget deficits had occurred in depression years such as the 1890s and 1907–1908. The largest deficits were associated with wars—the Civil War and World War I. In nondepression years, however, the federal government generally ran surpluses and paid off part of the debt created during the war years. The increase in the federal debt generated by the Civil War was reduced by 32 percent (in real terms) between 1865 and 1914. From 1920 to 1930, budget surpluses allowed the federal government to reduce by 24 percent the real debt created during World War I. Budget deficits reappeared in the 1930s. In the postwar years, as other economists developed and expanded on Keynes's new ideas, concerns with peacetime budget deficits were brushed aside as essentially unimportant. If it was necessary that the federal government run a deficit in order to keep the economy at full employment, so be it. As a consequence, between 1958 and 1997 the federal government ran deficits in every year except 1960 and 1969. The late 1990s finally brought the federal budget back to the point where surpluses and debt reduction could once again occur.

Although fiscal policy is no longer considered to be as powerful as it was thought to be in the twenty-five years following the end of World War II, many economists still consider it an important tool in stabilizing aggregate economic activity.

MONETARY POLICY AFTER THE GREAT DEPRESSION

Monetary policy is the other half of the twin tools of macroeconomic policy. The Great Depression also changed some of the goals of monetary policy—at least for several decades. Under the New Deal the Federal Reserve System was given the power to vary reserve requirements as an additional tool to exercise monetary policy. But the Fed's one attempt to use this tactic for short-term monetary policy, in 1936–1937, convinced it that varying reserve requirements was not useful for short-term stabilization policy, and it was not so used afterward.

The Fed's monetary policy decisions in the 1920s and 1930s were driven primarily by free reserves (or bank reserves in excess of what was required by bank deposits) and the level of interest rates. When free reserves increased, as they did in the late 1930s, and interest rates were low, monetary policy was "easy" or "expansionary." This method of determining monetary policy continued through the 1970s. The Great Depression did succeed in destroying the gold standard as a source of discipline on monetary policy. After World War II the Fed's operating strategy, based on free reserves and interest rates, tended to destabilize the economy and magnify price-level changes. Without the constraint of the gold standard, by the early 1960s the Fed had stumbled into an inflationary monetary policy. And this continued reliance on free reserves and levels of interest rates accelerated the rate of price inflation through the 1960s and 1970s. In October 1979 the Fed announced a significant change in its conduct of monetary policy in an attempt to remove the inflationary bias: it began targeting the growth of the monetary base (bank reserves and the cash held by the nonbanking public) rather than interest rates. Interest rates quickly shot up, and just as quickly the rate of price inflation began to fall. Although the Fed later relaxed this stance and began considering short-term interest rates in its decisions during the 1980s and 1990s, price inflation was considerably reduced.

GROWTH OF THE FEDERAL GOVERNMENT AND FEDERAL FISCALISM

The Great Depression resulted in a significant growth of federal government programs, including intervention in areas previously off limits. The Great Depression was much more severe than previous contractions and led to greater support for doing "something" (or "anything") to get the economy moving. Excluding its progressive wing, by the 1920s the Republican party tended to be a party of "small" government. During the 1920s debates about income tax rates, the Republicans, led by Andrew Mellon, had argued for reductions in income tax rates and reductions in federal government spending. By contrast, Democrats and progressive Republicans had argued for much smaller tax cuts targeted at lower-income taxpayers and for increases in federal government spending to utilize the large budget surpluses. Because Republicans controlled Congress and the White House, income tax rates were cut sharply during the 1920s and the federal government did not grow. Voters sent the Democrats into office to end the depression, and they took advantage of this mandate to begin expanding the role of the federal government. Roosevelt proved to be masterful in directing this expansion and developing a consensus to support it. This consensus lasted into the 1970s, when evidence began to accumulate that many of these government programs were not working.

Not only did the federal government grow relative to other governments and to the overall economy as a result of the depression, but it created a largely new federal fiscalism. Before the 1930s, federal grants averaged less than 2 percent of state and local government revenues. Because state and local governments did not depend on federal revenue sharing, they were for the most part independent of federal controls. By

1934 federal grants as a share of state and local revenue had climbed to 13.7 percent, and most of it came with strings attached. Although federal revenue sharing fell somewhat in the first decade after World War II, to 9 percent in the early 1950s, by 1977 it constituted nearly 25 percent of state and local government revenues. The struggle for control of New Deal programs between state and national governments and between the president and Congress led to the growth of federal revenue sharing as a means to control state and local government spending. Federal fiscalism has continued and grown since the New Deal. Without the Great Depression and New Deal it is doubtful that this lasting change in the structure of American government would have occurred.

Finally, the Great Depression ushered in a dramatic increase in the federal government's redistributive role, a role that had begun in 1913 with the passage of the federal personal income tax. The Fair Labor Standards Act of 1938, the first and second Agricultural Adjustment Acts, the National Industrial Recovery Act, and the Social Security Act that included unemployment insurance, aid to families with dependent children, old age assistance, and Social Security, as well as many other pieces of New Deal legislation, were designed to shift income away from higher earners and toward lower earners. The expansion of the federal government's redistributive role, begun in the New Deal, has continued to the present day.

GROWTH OF THE REGULATORY STATE

The 1930s saw a huge expansion of the regulatory powers and activities of the federal government. The door to this expansion had been opened with the passage of the 1887 Interstate Commerce Act to regulate railroads. But its full flowering did not occur until the 1930s when federal regulation was extended to interstate activities in trucking, busing, airlines, radio, power generation and transmission, oil and gas pipelines, securities exchanges, coal mining, agriculture, and other sectors. Agriculture provides an interesting case study of federal regulation because it is the foremost example of an industry that would otherwise be purely competitive. Agricultural product prices tend to be set in markets where individual farmers and buyers have virtually no personal influence over the price at which they sell and buy.

Before the 1930s there was relatively little federal intervention in agriculture. Today agriculture is one of the more highly regulated sectors of the American economy. Although in recent years the federal government has passed a "freedom to farm" act ostensibly aimed at reducing federal intervention in the agricultural sector, there is little evidence of such a withdrawal.

This is not to say that many farmers would not have welcomed some sort of federal intervention before the 1930s. Farmers led the way in the Populist revolts of the late nineteenth century, and in the 1920s they were vocal in demanding that the government do something to raise prices, particularly grain prices, reduce farm debt, and slow the decline of the farming sector. But most of the laws proposed to achieve such goals could not be passed. Before the 1930s most laws that were adopted to aid the farmer did so indirectly. These included reductions in tariffs on manufactured products, the regulation of railroad rates, food inspection to promote a greater demand for agricultural products, increases in the money supply to reduce agricultural prices, and the promotion of marketing and buying cooperatives. Some laws were aimed at aiding farmers in general by authorizing new Department of Agriculture agencies to conduct research into the control of animal and plant diseases as well as to examine soil conditions. Few of the laws related to increasing the demand for or restricting the supply of particular agricultural products—but from 1933 on, this is exactly what most federal laws did. Federal budget expenditures for the economic regulation of agricultural production became a fact of life during the New Deal. Since World War II the bulk of these expenditures have been for demand enhancement programs that make the federal government the buyer of last resort.

These agricultural programs have never been very focused. If they were intended to stop the long-term contraction of the agricultural sector, they have failed. If they were intended to allow small family farmers to earn enough to continue farming, they have failed. The bulk of subsidies have gone (and continue to go) to large, wealthy farmers, not small family farmers. Demand enhancing programs have led at times to immense stores of government purchased corn, wheat, dairy, and other agricultural commodities in attempts to keep prices higher than what would otherwise have prevailed and higher than world prices. These programs, which began under the New Deal, show no signs of abating today. The Great Depression provided a crisis that was large enough to justify politically the creation of agricultural regulatory policies on a scale never envisioned before 1930.

THE RISE OF SOCIAL WELFARE PROGRAMS

One of the most striking changes to emerge from the Great Depression decade was the rise of a set of government-sponsored social welfare programs. Not only were these programs much wider in scope than anything that had previously existed, they also moved the federal government into areas in which it had not been involved. These programs continued after World War II and eventually opened the door to the Kennedy-Johnson expansion of anti-poverty programs in the 1960s. Whether all of these social welfare programs were desirable can be debated. What is not debatable is the fact that the way we live, work, and retire was dramatically changed as a result of the enactment of these New Deal social welfare programs.

The four most important components of this social welfare legislation—old-age insurance, unemployment insurance, Aid to Families with Dependent Children (AFDC), and Old Age Assistance (old-age pensions)—were tied together into one bill. In mid-1934, Roosevelt estimated that unemployment insurance could be more easily passed than Social Security, old-age assistance, and other types of safety-net legislation. An unemployment insurance bill, known as the Wagner-Lewis bill, had been introduced in Congress earlier in 1934, but Roosevelt asked that it be deferred. He then created the Committee on Economic Security, chaired by the secretary of labor, Frances Perkins, to look into all aspects of social insurance. The committee developed the omnibus Social Security Act.

Unemployment Insurance

The United States was slow in adopting unemployment insurance, as well as other social welfare programs, compared with most European nations. It has been argued that unemployment insurance would ultimately have been adopted in the United States even in the absence of the Great Depression because of the precedent set by European countries. But the depression made this question moot. The rise of massive unemployment among individuals who clearly desired to work but simply could not find a job served as the focal point for the crusade for unemployment insurance. Only three states had introduced unemployment insurance bills before the Great Depression—Massachusetts in 1916 and New York and Wisconsin in 1921—and four others had considered such legislation in 1929—Connecticut, Minnesota, Pennsylvania, and South Carolina. In 1932, Wisconsin was the first to pass such a bill. As the depression deepened, more states considered this action, and some federal bills were proposed.

As adopted, unemployment insurance in the United States differed from that in most other countries. In most nations this protection is a central government program, but in the United States it is a joint federal-state initiative. It is also somewhat less generous, and the benefits are available for a shorter duration than generally is the case elsewhere. Unemployment insurance in the United States also differs in its basis in "experience rating" (or "merit rating" as it was called in the 1930s). Those who wrote the legislation believed that to some extent firms could reduce seasonal unemployment, and this was a major aim of the new law. Firms whose employees became unemployed more frequently were taxed at higher rates. In many countries all firms were taxed at a common rate, with the tax revenues placed in a common pool from which all unemployed workers drew their compensation. The evidence does suggest that unemployment insurance in the United States has reduced seasonal unemployment.

Unemployment insurance, more than most other social welfare programs enacted in the 1930s, has remained largely unchanged. It has been extended to industries not covered in the original 1935 legislation, and the level of payments has increased. But the joint federal-state structure, the "experience rating," and limitations on the duration of payments are all essentially the same as provided in the original legislation.

OLD AGE ASSISTANCE AND AFDC

Both Old Age Assistance and Aid to Families with Dependent Children (AFDC) were also joint federal-state programs. The AFDC program was a means to ensure that children did not suffer because of the poverty of a deserving widow. Federal funds were distributed by state agencies. When old-age insurance—what today is referred to as Social Security—was passed, it was anticipated that for some years most of the elderly would not be eligible. To bridge this period, Old Age Assistance was created to provide basic incomes for the elderly who were unable to work and not eligible for Social Security. This was also a joint federal-state program with funds provided by the federal government and distributed, according to federal rules, by state agencies. As late as 1950, Old Age Assistance remained a larger program than Social Security, but as more and more of the elderly became eligible for Social Security, the program shrank. In 1972, Congress replaced all of the federal-state Old Age Assistance programs with a fully federally funded and administered Supplemental Security Income program. The SSI program continued to be funded from general revenues rather than from payroll taxes collected through the Social Security administration.

SOCIAL SECURITY

The cornerstone of the social welfare programs created under the New Deal was Old Age Insurance (OAI or Social Security). Unlike the other three parts of the Social Security Act, this program was funded from its own taxes and administered completely by the federal government. As was the case with the other programs, the United States was relatively late among developed countries in establishing an Old Age Insurance program. Initially the program was designed to be actuarially sound, with each person paying in to establish a retirement fund from which he or she could later draw. The income limit on contributions and the method of paying out social insurance to the elderly did create some income redistribution. But by 1939, Washington politicians decided that payments had to be made much sooner. The goal of fully funding the Social Security program was removed, and the program became primarily a "pay-as-you-go" transfer program, transferring income (through Social Security taxes) from the working population to the retired elderly.

Although the designers of Social Security anticipated that the program would grow and taxes rise, they underestimated the magnitude of the plan in two ways. First, they anticipated that a much larger trust fund would be accumulated, and, second, they underestimated how much the average life span would increase. Social Security has continued to be altered since the end of the 1930s. In 1939 the benefits of the program were extended to both spouses and to widows of retired workers. In 1950 benefits were extended to dependents of retired workers. In 1965, Congress added disability benefits for workers under sixty-five and hospital benefits for those over sixty-five. Payroll taxes were increased so as to fund these extensions, and the program became known as OASDHI (Old Age, Survivors, Disability and Hospital Insurance). Insurance for physicians and surgeons was separately funded. The combined insurance programs became known as Medicare.

Recently Social Security has generated considerable controversy. Without a significant trust fund, it has always been a largely pay-as-you-go program. This did not prove difficult when there were eight to nine workers actively paying in Social Security taxes to fund each retired worker drawing on the program. But Congress has increased the real benefits to retired workers, and, with an aging population, the number of active workers paying taxes compared to each retiree has been falling. Currently there are about three workers for each retiree, and the Social Security tax burden has been rising. As this ratio continues to decline, either the Social Security tax burden per worker will have to rise or the benefits for each retiree will have to be reduced. There are no easy choices. The

Social Security program and its problems are clearly a legacy of the Great Depression.

INTERNATIONAL TRADE AND FINANCE

In the aftermath of the Great Depression, U.S. international economic relations were transformed. As the most powerful economy on earth, its decisions could not help but influence all the other market economies. Tariff reductions were the first evidence of this impact.

Between the Civil War and the Hawley-Smoot Tariff of 1930, Congress retained the exclusive authority to determine tariffs. Although Republicans and Democrats differed over the size of tariffs, they agreed that tariffs were a congressional prerogative. The Great Depression ushered in tariff increases across the globe, particularly in protective tariffs designed to aid domestic producers. In retaliation, other countries passed or increased their own protective tariffs. The new Congress brought in with the 1932 elections decided that it would be easier for the president to obtain mutual tariff reductions—to increase American exports—through bilateral or multilateral negotiations. In 1934 the president was granted the authority to reach tariff reduction agreements with foreign nations (without requiring congressional approval) in the Reciprocal Trade Agreement Act. This act allowed the president to conduct bilateral and multilateral negotiations. The RTAA has continued to be the basis of U.S. foreign trade policy and has helped bring about significant declines in tariffs rates since the 1930s.

The reconstituted gold exchange system of the 1920s had ignited the worldwide Great Depression. By 1933 most countries had left the gold standard. Internally the United States went off the gold standard in 1933, and even France abandoned it in the late 1930s. The United States remained on the gold standard externally with a devalued dollar. As noted earlier, the devaluation and growing clouds of war led to a huge flow of gold into the United States.

After the war, countries again tried to reestablish a fixed exchange rate international monetary system. The United States defined its dollar in gold at $35 an ounce and stood ready to redeem dollars for gold with the central banks of the other nations. Other countries defined their currencies with a fixed exchange rate against the dollar. At home, American citizens continued to be prohibited from owning monetary gold. This system, named the Bretton Woods system after the site of an international monetary conference, initially worked well, but as time passed the inflexibility of exchange rates presented growing problems. The United States generally had somewhat higher rates of price inflation than Germany and some other European nations. When American corporations began to buy foreign firms, foreign securities, and foreign resources, these large capital imports led to a persistent flow of dollars out of the United States while Germany and, to a lesser extent, France enjoyed surpluses in their trade balances. The fixed exchange rates could not easily be adjusted to offset these changes, and gold flows no longer worked to alter domestic price levels.

As the rate of price inflation in the United States increased at the end of the 1960s, other countries became less and less willing to hold American dollars. Some countries, especially France, began systematically to redeem dollars for gold. As U.S. gold reserves dwindled, policymakers were faced with two fundamental choices: they could take serious steps to reduce the rate of price inflation in the United States, or devalue the dollar. Reducing the money supply to stop price inflation (in the face of the loss of gold reserves) was never a serious option. On August 15, 1971, President Richard M. Nixon devalued the dollar as part of a program of domestic inflation-fighting policies. Nixon's move shocked the international monetary system because its entire scheme of fixed exchange rates was predicated on the dollar's fixed exchange rate with gold. Early in 1973 the dollar was again devalued, and in March 1973 the United States, and the world, adopted a system of floating exchange rates as the United States stopped redeeming dollars for gold. Released from the last constraint of a gold standard, the Federal Reserve System stumbled into increasingly inflationary monetary policies in the 1970s. Not until the 1980s did the Fed finally begin to control its money creation and develop new guidelines for conducting monetary policy.

The postwar Bretton Woods system of fixed exchange rates and capital account restrictions was not consistent with growing capital flows, and as a consequence through the 1950s and 1960s these flows remained below the levels of the turn of the century and the 1920s. With the introduction of floating exchange rates in the 1970s, international capital flows began growing; by the 1990s they were relatively as large as those at the turn of the century.

Although the Great Depression brought in a new policy regime that led to significant declines in tariff rates, it is not clear that the gold standard would have survived even in the absence of the Great Depression. The fixed exchange rate gold standard and floating exchange rates are alternative price mechanisms for balancing international trade in commodities, services, and capital. With fixed exchange rates, international gold flows lead to changes in domestic money supplies and price levels to balance international exchanges. With floating exchange rates, changes in the value of a country's currency relative to other countries' currencies provide the balancing mechanism. A gold standard provides a constraint on the propensity of central bankers to create money, and the fixed exchange rates provide a friendlier environment for long-term international capital flows. The scheme works as long as governments are willing to abide by the rules of the gold standard and not manage money supplies, price levels, and international reserves for domestic purposes. By the late nineteenth century, however, governments were increasingly interfering with international trade in pursuit of domestic agendas. The restored gold standard of the 1920s was never allowed to function as it was supposed to. Pursuing domestic agendas, countries manipulated trade, money supplies, and international reserves. Thus the gold standard of the 1920s was doomed, as was the postwar Bretton Woods system with its fixed exchange rates. In addition, both in the 1920s as well as in the postwar era the world supply of gold did not grow as fast as world production. A gold standard in the postwar era would likely have fared no different than in the 1920s. As long as countries were not willing to tolerate the required price deflation and its costs, an increasing demand for gold reserves would have brought on the same kind of crisis in the postwar era as had occurred in the 1920s.

COULD IT HAPPEN AGAIN?

Was the Great Depression a unique event? Could we have a repeat of 1929–1933 and the slow recovery of the New Deal years? These are difficult questions. The United States had experienced contractions before the Great Depression— in 1873–1878, 1895–1896, 1907–1908, 1920–1921—as well as after—in 1937–1938, the minor contractions of 1948–1949, 1953–1954, 1960–1961, and 1970–1971, the more serious contractions of 1974–1975 and 1981–1982, and the less serious one of 1990–1991. Thus we certainly have not eliminated the contraction in economic activity. But since World War II the contractions have been milder and have been called "recessions," so as to not associate them with the Great Depression of

1929–1933. In the most serious postwar recession, in 1981–1982, the severity of the downturn approached the severity of the 1937–1938 depression. This provides some hope that we have learned something from the 1930s.

And we believe that we have gained some understanding of how to use economic policies to reduce the severity and length of contractions. We assume this even though inappropriate monetary policy brought on the 1981–1982 recession. But we take comfort in the thought that we now know how to exercise expansionary fiscal policy, and we know that the Federal Reserve System is able to exercise an expansionary monetary policy even in a severe contraction. Thus we should be able to prevent contractions from being long and severe by the careful use of countercyclical macroeconomic policies. Still, our continued inability to develop econometric models that can accurately predict contractions means that we will not be free of them.

We also know more than we used to about the effects of international economic policies. The switch from fixed exchange rates under a gold standard (of some sort) to floating exchange rates has reduced the likelihood of the initiation of a worldwide depression such as occurred at the end of the 1920s. But the increasingly interdependent economies that have resulted from the rise of global business means that events in one country have a greater impact in other countries. For example, the Southeastern Asian financial crisis at the end of the 1990s affected many other countries around the world.

Finally, the 1930s are not a testimonial to the fundamental problems of market-oriented economies, as some have argued. Events following World War II have shown that market societies can easily outperform managed economies. What failed in the 1930s were *governments*, in their eagerness to direct activity to achieve political ends—ends that were often contradictory. Attempts to stop international financial markets from working through the gold standard brought on the depression. Government efforts to combat the depression by fixing wage rates and supporting agricultural prices, and the ineptness of the Federal Reserve's monetary policy, made the depression much longer and more severe in the United States. Government attempts to reshape American society to fit the visions of a new administration and Congress made the recovery agonizingly slow and in 1937–1938 helped create a depression within a depression. It has taken us a long time to begin to understand these costly lessons of the 1930s.

Ultimately, however, there are no guarantees. We must assume that the increasing wisdom of those in charge of economic policies helps them make correct decisions. A study of economic history can help us understand what we should, and should not, do in order to promote stability and growth. But no one can guarantee that policymakers will take advantage of the lessons of history.

A Note on Sources

THERE IS an enormous literature examining the Great Depression; no more than a sample of it can be noted here.

One of the more recent surveys of the interwar period is Peter Fearon, *War, Prosperity & Depression: The U.S. Economy, 1917–1945* (Lawrence, Kans., 1987). This period is also described in Gene Smiley, *The American Economy in the Twentieth Century* (Cincinnati, 1994). Older but still useful detailed surveys can be found in George Soule, *Prosperity Decade: From War to Depression, 1917–1929* (New York, 1947), and Broadus Mitchell, *Depression Decade: From New Era Through New Deal, 1929–1941* (New York, 1947). One of the best surveys of the 1930s is Lester V. Chandler, *America's Greatest Depression, 1928–1941* (New York, 1970). Other good surveys include Derek Aldcroft, *From Versailles to Wall Street, 1919–1929* (Berkeley, 1977), Charles Kindleberger, *The World in Depression, 1929–1939* (Berkeley, 1973), and Alan Milward, *War, Economy, and Society, 1939–1945* (Berkeley, 1977). Thomas Hall and J. David Ferguson's recent survey of the Great Depression, *The Great Depression: An International Disaster of Perverse Economic Policies* (Ann Arbor, 1998), is fairly technical and requires a more advanced knowledge of economic theory.

Several studies have pointed to the international character of the Great Depression and its roots in the dislocations of World War I and the reconstituted gold exchange standard of the 1920s. Charles Kindleberger, in *The World in Depression, 1929–1939*, had an early explanation of the international character of the contraction. More recently Peter Temin's study, *Lessons from the Great Depression* (Cambridge, Mass., 1989) and Part 2 in David Glasner's *Free Banking and Monetary Reform* (New York, 1989) both present the modern explanation for the initiation of the worldwide Great Depression. The most complete exposition of this thesis, and one that I have drawn on heavily in this study, is by Barry Eichengreen, *Golden Fetters: The Gold Standard and the Great Depression, 1919–1939* (New York, 1992).

Although various aspects of their analysis have been criticized, chapters 7–9 of Milton Friedman and Anna Jacobson Schwartz's classic study *A Monetary History of the United States, 1867–1960* (Princeton, 1963) remain the starting point for studying the Great Depression and the recovery in the 1930s. Peter Temin's criticism of the monetarist explanation of the beginning of the severe downturn in 1930 must be examined—*Did Monetary Forces Cause the Great Depression?* (New York, 1976). On the role of the 1929 stock market crash in accelerating the initial decline, see Christina D. Romer, "The Great Crash and the Onset of the Great Depression," *Quarterly Journal of Economics,* 105 (August 1990), 597–624, and Frederic S. Mishkin, "The Household Balance Sheet and the Great Depression," *Journal of Economic History*, 38 (December 1978), 918–937. On the role of wage rigidity in making the depression more severe, see Murray N. Rothbard, *America's Great Depression* (Kansas City, 1963) for an earlier exposition, though Irving Bernstein in *The Lean Years: A History of the American Worker, 1920–1933* (Boston, 1960) has a contrary view. Anthony Patrick O'Brien presents a behavioral explanation for the wage rigidity in "A Behavioral Explanation for Nominal Wage Rigidity During the Great Depression," *Quarerly Journal of Economics,* 104 (November 1989), 719–735, and this subject is examined in detail in Richard K. Vedder and Lowell P. Gallaway, *Out of Work: Unemployment and Government in Twentieth-Century America* (New York, 1993).

Federal Reserve System policy during the contraction has received extensive scrutiny. In addition to Friedman and Schwartz, *A Monetary History of the United States*, and Eichengreen, *Golden Fetters*, see Karl Brunner, ed., *The Great Depression Revisited* (Boston, 1981); Lester Chandler, *American Monetary Policy, 1928–1941* (New York, 1971); Gary M. Anderson, William F. Shughart II, and Robert D. Tollison, "A Public Choice Theory of the Great Depression," *Public Choice,* 59 (October 1988), 3–23; Karl Brunner and Allen Meltzer, "What Did We Learn from the Monetary Experience of the United States in the Great Depression?" *Canadian Journal of Economics,* 1 (May 1968), 334–348; Charles W. Calomiris, "Financial Factors in the Great Depression," *Journal of Economic Perspectives,* 7 (Spring 1993), 61–86; Gerald Epstein and Thomas Ferguson, "Monetary Policy, Loan Liquidation, and Industrial Conflict: The Federal Reserve and Open Market Operations of 1932," *Journal of Economic History,* 44 (December 1984), 975–984; Alexander J. Field, "A New Interpretation of the Onset of the Great Depression," *Journal of Economic History,* 44 (June 1984), 489–498; Paul B. Trescott, "Federal Reserve Policy in the Great Contraction: A Counterfactual Assessment," *Explorations in Economic History,* 19 (July 1982), 211–220; David C. Wheelock, "The Strategy, Effectiveness, and Consistency of Federal Reserve Monetary Policy, 1924–1933," *Explorations in Economic History,* 26 (October 1989), 453–476; Eugene N. White, "A Reinterpretation of the Banking Crisis of 1930," *Journal of Economic History,* 44 (March 1984), 119–138; Elmus Wicker, "Federal Reserve Monetary Policy, 1922–1933: A Reinterpretation," *Journal of Political Economy,* 73 (August 1965), 325–343; Elmus Wicker, "A Reconsideration of the Causes of the Banking Panic of 1930," *Explorations in Economic History,* 40 (September 1980), 571–583; and Elmus Wicker, *The Banking Panics of the Great Depression* (New York, 1996). For one explanation of the end of the contraction, see Peter Temin and Barrie Wigmore, "The End of One Big Deflation," *Explorations in Economic History,* 27 (October 1990), 483–502.

The New Deal also has an extensive literature, some of which considers the entire 1933 to 1940 period as the New Deal rather than breaking this up into a first and a second New Deal. One of the best analyses of the New Deal is Ellis Hawley, *The New Deal and the Problem of Monopoly, 1933–1939* (Princeton, 1965). Paul Conkin's short study *The New Deal,* 3rd ed. (Wheeling, Ill., 1992) is still valuable, as is the more recent study by Colin Gordon, *New Deals: Business, Labor, and Politics in America, 1920–1935*

(New York, 1994). Another book from which I have drawn extensively is Gary Dean Best, *Pride, Prejudice, and Politics: Roosevelt versus Recovery, 1933–1938* (New York, 1991). In addition, the following studies should be consulted: Jim F. Couch and William F. Shugart II, *The Political Economy of the New Deal* (Northampton, Mass., 1998); Robert Higgs, *Crisis and Leviathan: Critical Episodes in the Growth of American Government* (New York, 1987); Robert F. Himmelberg, *The Origins of the National Recovery Administration: Business, Government, and the Trade Association Issue, 1921–1933* (New York, 1976); Vedder and Gallaway, *Out of Work*; Jonathan Hughes, "Roots of Regulation: The New Deal," in Gary M. Walton, ed., *Regulatory Change in an Atmosphere of Crisis: Current Implications of the Roosevelt Years* (New York, 1979); Bradford A. Lee, "The New Deal Reconsidered," *Wilson Quarterly*, 6 (Spring 1982), 62–76; William E. Leuchtenburg, "The New Deal and the Analogue of War," in John Braeman, et al., *Change and Continuity in Twentieth Century America* (New York, 1967): Michael Weinstein, *Recovery and Redistribution Under the NIRA* (Amsterdam, 1980); Wilson D. Miscamble, "Thurman Arnold Goes to Washington: A Look at Antitrust Policy in the Later New Deal," *Business History Review*, 56 (Spring 1982), 295–304; Don C. Reading, "New Deal Activity and the States, 1933 to 1939," *Journal of Economic History*, 33 (December 1973), 792–810; John Joseph Wallis, "The Political Economy of New Deal Spending Revisited, Again: With and Without Nevada," *Explorations in Economic History*, 35 (April 1998), 140–170; Gavin Wright, "The Political Economy of New Deal Spending: An Econometric Analysis," *Review of Economics and Statistics*, 56 (February 1974), 30–38; Michael Darby, "Three-and-a-Half Million Employees Have Been Mislaid: Or, An Explanation of Unemployment, 1934–1941," *Journal of Political Economy*, 84 (February 1976), 1–16; and Jonathan R. Kesselman and N. E. Savin, "Three-and-a-Half Million Workers Never Were Lost," *Economic Inquiry*, 16 (April 1978), 205–225.

On the depression of 1937–1938 see Friedman and Schwartz, *A Monetary History*; Benjamin M. Anderson, *Economics and the*

Public Welfare: A Financial and Economic History of the United States (New York, 1949); Melvin D. Brockie, "Theories of the 1937–1938 Depression," *Economic Journal*, 60 (1950), 292–310; E. Cary Brown, "Fiscal Policy in the Thirties: A Reappraisal," *American Economic Review*, 46 (December 1956), 357–879; Alvin H. Hansen, *Full Recovery or Stagnation* (New York, 1938); Larry Peppers, "Full-Employment Surplus Analysis and Structural Change: The 1930s," *Explorations in Economic History*, 10 (Winter 1973), 197–210; Kenneth D. Roose, *The Economics of Recession and Revival: An Interpretation of 1937–38* (New Haven, 1954); Thomas M. Renaghan, "A New Look at Fiscal Policy in the 1930s," *Research in Economic History*, 11 (1988), 171–183; Vedder and Gallaway, *Out of Work;* Gene Smiley, "Some Austrian Perspectives on Keynesian Fiscal Policy and the Recovery in the Thirties," *Review of Austrian Economics*, 1 (1987), 145–180; Darby, "Three-and-a-Half Million U.S. Employees Have Been Mislaid"; and Peter Temin, "Socialism and Wages in the Recovery from the Great Depression in the United States and Germany," *Journal of Economic History*, 50 (June 1990), 297–308.

Several studies address the lagging recovery from the Great Depression. On the persistence of unemployment, see Darby, "Three-and-a-Half Million U.S. Employees Have Been Mislaid," and two papers by Robert Margo, "The Microeconomics of Depression Unemployment," *Journal of Economic History*, 51 (June 1991), 333–342, and "Employment and Unemployment in 1930s," *Journal of Economic Perspectives*, 7 (Spring 1993), 41–60. Problems with generating sufficient private-sector investment are addressed in Michael Bernstein, "A Reassessment of Investment Failure in the Interwar American Economy," *Journal of Economic History*, 44 (June 1984), 479–488; Bernstein's thesis is developed in greater detail in *The Great Depression, Delayed Recovery and Economic Change in America, 1929–1939* (New York, 1987). The problems of resurrecting residential housing investment in the 1930s are addressed in Alexander J. Field, "Uncontrolled Land Development and the Duration of the Depression in the United States," *Journal of Economic History*, 52 (December

1992), 785–805. In this study I have relied heavily on Robert Higgs's study, "Regime Uncertainty: Why the Great Depression Lasted So Long and Why Prosperity Returned After the War," *Independent Review*, 1 (Spring 1997), 561–590.

Both Robert Higgs in *Crisis and Leviathan* and Richard Vedder and Lowell Gallaway in *Out of Work* address the question of economic recovery during World War II. I have relied primarily on Robert Higgs, "Wartime Prosperity? A Reassessment of the U.S. Economy in the 1940s." *Journal of Economic History,* 52 (March 1992), 41–60, in assessing the recovery from the depression between 1941 and 1945. But a concurring opinion on the importance of the immediate post-1945 period can also be found in Richard K. Vedder and Lowell Gallaway, "The Great Depression of 1946," *Review of Austrian Economics*, 5 (1991), 3–32. Finally, I have relied on a series of papers in Michael D. Bordo, Claudia Goldin, and Eugene N. White, ed., *The Defining Moment: The Great Depression and the American Economy in the Twentieth Century* (Chicago, 1998), in examining the legacy of the Great Depression.

Index

A NOTE ON THE AUTHOR

Gene Smiley was born in Coin, Iowa, and studied at the University of Iowa, where he received B.A., M.A., and Ph.D. degrees. Since 1973 he has taught at Marquette University, where he is professor of economics. He has written widely on economic theory, American economic history, and Austrian economics, and is the author of *The American Economy in the Twentieth Century*. He lives in Waukesha, Wisconsin.